Awakening the Giant

Awakening the Giant

*Evangelism and
the Catholic Church*

PAT LYNCH

*Foreword by
Mervyn Alexander, Bishop of Clifton*

Darton, Longman and Todd
London

First published in 1990 by
Darton, Longman and Todd Ltd
89 Lillie Road, London SW6 1UD

British Library Cataloguing in Publication Data

Lynch, Pat
  Awakening the giant.
  1. Catholic Church. Evangelism
  I. Title
  269′.2

  ISBN 0–232–51866–1

Phototypeset by Input Typesetting Ltd, London SW19 8DR
Printed and bound in Great Britain by
Courier International Ltd, Tiptree, Essex

Dedicated with love to my father (deceased),
my mother, brothers and sister, who were my
first teachers about God

Contents

Foreword

In some ways it is strange to have a 'Decade of Evangelization'. What else is the Church for? However we all need reminding from time to time of the fundamental mission and purpose of the Church.

A Christian is meant to be an outgoing person. Christ spent many years working quietly as a carpenter, and so proclaimed the holiness of the domestic church and of ordinary work. However, when the time was ripe, Christ stepped out of the shadows and began his personal evangelization of Galilee.

From the early days he drew others to share in the proclamation of the Good News. It was not to be a solo effort, a magnificent demonstration of his personal power. Instead he sent out some of his disciples on missionary journeys, and they came back rejoicing at the signs of power that had accompanied their preaching. There were also some women who accompanied him on his journeys and whose fidelity shone out at the time of his cross and resurrection. From the beginning it was clear that his whole company, his Church, was to be involved in evangelization. Every Christian is to be transformed by the Gospel in order to share the gift with others.

In the apostolic era men and women were associated with the apostles in presenting the Good News to others. So we see Priscilla and Aquila instructing Apollos. The newly baptized became new missionaries. That is how it ought to be. We can all think of impressive evangelistic campaigns in later Christian history.

It has been said recently that Europe is now mission territory needing a fresh evangelization. In ecumenical circles there is much discussion of the academic questions and the practical means. What is meant by evangelization? How does it relate to evangelism? What is mission? What are the ecumenical prospects and can we reach ecumenically acceptable definitions?

How can Christians co-operate in this work? What are the means available? Shall we see an expansion in Europe of radio and television evangelism? Is the personal, one-to-one approach the most effective?

In this book Father Lynch, an experienced evangelist, looks at questions of this kind in considerable depth. More than this, he reflects upon the content of evangelism, the basic elements of faith and how to present them. He considers the foundations of the biblical concept of conversion. He studies the 'master plan' of Jesus and shows how it can be followed today. He examines the place of prayer and the use of the Scriptures. Realistically he analyses the stumbling blocks in our society and asserts the universal need for evangelization. I believe that his concept of a community evangelizing a community is very important. He concludes on an optimistic note, offering various practical ways of evangelizing.

This is a timely book that will provoke much discussion and will encourage reflection and action in this crucial aspect of Church life. Is the future to be vitality or exhaustion?

Mervyn Alexander
Bishop of Clifton

Acknowledgements

It could be said that every book has many other authors. This is especially true when the setting is evangelization. I would like to express my thanks to all those people who helped me in my early ministry as a priest and, in particular, to my bishop, James McGuinness of Nottingham, for releasing me to be a full-time evangelist. This book has grown out of my work within the Catholic Church and my deepest desire to see her renewed.

There are many people who aided me in the writing of this book – Michelle Moran, Pat McGee, Fr Johnny Doherty, Fr Peter Tierney, Andrew Lowe, Andy Seweryn, Dave Burnett, Charles Whitehead and the Revd Eric Delve, to mention but a few.

I cannot sufficiently express my thanks to the priests, sisters, men and women of Sion Community for Evangelism who have inspired me over the years by their untiring dedication and self-sacrifice in proclaiming the 'Good News'. I feel privileged to be in their midst.

I am grateful to my secretary, Audrey Gibbs, who for a long time now has been somehow able to decipher my writing and put it into a meaningful typescript. The Sisters of Mercy, at Oldham, had to live with me while this book was being written; they know how thrilled I am to have had their support.

My editors at Darton Longman and Todd, Teresa de Bertodano and Morag Reeve, have given me steady personal support. Their warm encouragement and competent assistance helped me bring order to this book. Fr Michael Simpson SJ also added suggestions to my ardour and whatever qualities this book possesses stem from his subtle suggestions – such as, 'This sentence needs to be changed'.

All quotations in this publication are from the Jerusalem Bible, published and copyrighted 1966, 1967, 1968 by Darton Longman and Todd Ltd and Doubleday and Co. Inc.

Introduction

Evangelization is, today, a misunderstood word in many quarters of the Catholic Church. I have tried in this book to show that it is central to the Church's mission; it is her desire and driving force to evangelize. We must evangelize as Church. The living God can dwell in people's lives and transform society. We all as individuals need to be constantly evangelized so that a de-Christianized Europe can be Christian again. It is from this position of discovery and confidence that I write.

I was born into a Catholic family, where God was part of the family in a simple, down-to-earth way. My parents had great faith in God. They were uneducated; in fact, like most people of their generation, they could barely read or write. Yet they possessed qualities which cannot be gleaned from books. They brought me up in an atmosphere where prayer and going to Mass were vitally important. God was constantly holding on to me. There was a part of me wanting to throw off the 'traditional' image of Catholicism, yet I knew that God wanted me to be a priest. My search through philosophy and theology brought me more head-knowledge, but there was a hunger deep down for more. I know that I had gone as far as I could in trying to reach God by pure reason. Something had to happen in my life to convince me of the special relationship between God and me. I made one simple prayer, 'Lord, if you are real, touch my life with your Spirit.' After a time an almost imperceptible breeze of fresh air began to clear away the dust and dry leaves in my faith-life. God was building on what had already been planted. I was being evangelized and began to

1

understand that becoming a Christian means to have God live in us. But I was a Catholic from birth. I didn't have gigantic problems in my life, yet I needed a new conversion. Being converted anew didn't take me away from the Catholic Church but made me more convinced of everything I had been taught. It is so important for us to open our hearts and minds to the Holy Spirit.

We all know that God does not do things for our selfish reasons. He evangelizes people for ministry. I remember that on my ordination day the bishop handed me a Bible saying, 'Proclaim the Good News.' Preaching the Good News is the priority of any priest. I was doing this already. How was it going to change? The parish, in which I was a curate, began to grow, rapidly, and I was being asked to speak nationally and internationally. Evangelism was at the core of my being. Through a lot of circumstances over the years, my bishop finally released me to form a new community with the specific charism of evangelism. My dream of helping to breathe new life into the Catholic Church was realized in the formation of Sion Community for Evangelism. Priests, sisters and lay people began to join me in the common vision which was being put forward by the Church. We are only one group of people trying to put the exhortations of Vatican II and the Church's teaching on evangelization into action. I know that there are many others.

Having given you a glimpse of where I have come from, I want to assert that this book has grown out of experience. I know, now, that conversion is possible for ordinary people. I have seen it happen, not at the level of theory but in a very practical way. Evangelization does work. I have decided to write on paper my deepest aspirations to see a Catholic Church renewed through evangelism.

This book is an exhortation to act. I realize that it is not complete in itself but, hopefully, it is the first of many more books dedicated to this vital subject. Even if only one section stimulates the reader, then it has been worthwhile in breaking this new ground. This book is intended as a study of 'initiation', it will introduce the reader to the 'Decade of Evangelization 1990–2000'. Finally, I do not wish it to be considered as a scientific study but rather as an extended 'working paper' on the subject of evangelization.

I would like this book to be of help primarily to bishops, priests, religious, and lay leaders in the Church. I also include all other interested people who may find it helpful and stimulating. One of my greatest desires is that this book will create an informative bridge between the Catholic Church and the evangelical Churches. I realize that a number of good books on evangelism have been written in the Protestant tradition, and I am grateful for such works. In Catholicism we have been lacking in this field. Through the pages of this book may the Catholic perspective on evangelism be shown. Nowhere am I attempting to score points; the issue of evangelism is too serious for that trivial kind of treatment.

While revising the original manuscript I have seen glaring omissions, scanty references to big themes and a degree of personal ignorance on some of the crucial issues facing us. Yet as we evangelize, during the coming Decade of Evangelization, we can grow and learn from each other.

Finally, throughout this book I inter-change the words 'evangelism' and 'evangelization' for effect. There is also a certain amount of repetition in this work which will serve to emphasize the points I am making. My aim is to initiate my readers into an understanding of evangelism and the Catholic Church. They will be able to see that what I have written is not just my own idealism but authenticated Catholic teaching. Over the years, as a Catholic evangelist, I have been constantly evangelized and changed. My faith has been broadened by the many situations I have met. What I have to say in the following chapters comes from personal experience and the experience of Sion Community to which I am privileged to belong. I am proud to be called an evangelist, a Christian and a Catholic. Welcome to this book, *Awakening the Giant*. Welcome to evangelism and the Catholic Church.

1

A Church Reconstructed

To evangelize is Catholic

Recently I was giving a talk in a Catholic parish. Near the end of the evening a man stood up and asked me, 'Father, do you have a parish?' I answered 'No'. 'Well then,' he said, 'what exactly do you do?' 'I am a Catholic evangelist,' I replied. 'But that's a contradiction in terms. How can you be a Catholic and an evangelist? I thought that it was only Protestants who were evangelists,' he retorted. On that particular evening I thought I was extremely Catholic, not least in the fact that I was wearing my clerical suit and my Roman collar. But the reaction of my friend is very common in Catholic circles. Evangelism is not seen as particularly Catholic; we tend to think of it as a Protestant word. It is also a very misunderstood word, suggesting Billy Graham meetings, telly-evangelists, people who have a big name and big meetings, slick preachers in well-pressed suits or even mass hysteria.

Yet to evangelize is central to the Catholic Church and its tradition. People like St Patrick and St Augustine, to mention but two, were evangelists. The whole teaching of the Catholic Church, spanning the last 2,000 years, is orientated towards evangelism.

The decree *Ad Gentes Divinitus* came into existence to confront the Church again with its missionary nature. 'So that the whole Church becomes Missionary . . . and the entire people of God be made aware of its missionary obligations.[1] Or again, 'We wish to confirm once more that the task of evangelizing

5

all peoples constitutes the essential mission of the Church . . . Evangelizing is in fact the grace and vocation proper to the Church, her deepest identity. She exists in order to evangelize.[2]

Having said all this I am aware that words can be much misunderstood. The use of language is sensitive, and words can have religious overtones and affiliations. Twenty years ago 'evangelize' was not a Catholic word; it was Protestant and smacked of fundamentalism. We were more at home with the word 'convert'. The reason for this was the fact that for us the words 'Kingdom' and 'Church' were almost synonymous. We had a legacy of theology handed down to us from people, like St Augustine, who assumed that when we were converted to Jesus we were also converted to the Church. We thought that we possessed the 'absolute' when it came to faith. Nowadays people are quite open about their desire for God but retain second thoughts about the Church as an institution. I believe the reason for this has been the changes in world history since World War II, resulting in the chain reaction of the Second Vatican Council. In Pope Pius XII's reign an ecclesiastical style was brought to an end, and a new understanding of Kingdom and Church was inaugurated by Pope John XXIII. The new climate since World War II demanded new answers, even of the Church. In this climate of openness we have been more ready to learn from our Protestant brothers and sisters, and part of that learning process is a new understanding of evangelism.

I was giving a mission in Ireland, last year, and during one of my talks I asked the people to become a missionary church. One lady came up afterwards and said to me, 'Father, you are asking us to turn turtle, because in the past all the Church asked of us was to turn up, pay up and shut up.' I do appreciate that we (in particular bishops, priests and religious) moulded our people into what they are today. Now we are asking for a redirection and I know it will take time. We engaged our people, in the past, in a very private faith, and now we are asking them to have a direct witnessing faith. Yet as we embrace the whole concept of evangelization we, as a Church, have to take on a 'Star Trek' mentality and be energized so as to possess the evangelical mission. We need to shake off any paralysing complacency as we realize God's plans for self-revelation. We cannot afford to be naive in our attitude and practice in what lies ahead for our Church here in the Western world.

So the whole *raison d'être* of the Catholic (Christian) Church is to spread the gospel message. The message came before the Church, it was out of the Good News being received and accepted that the Church came into existence. 'The Church is born of the evangelizing activity of Jesus and the twelve,' says Pope Paul VI.[3] When this is lived in reality the ministry of evangelism does not consist in making the right noises and distributing graces but in effecting fellowship in Christ. By its very essence this will attract others. Therefore we can say that to be Catholic and an evangelizer is correct. To write or expound anything different would be a contradiction in terms.

What is evangelism?

Recently I was privileged in being asked to attend a two-day seminar on Renewal and Church Growth at Birmingham. There were people present representing England, Wales, Scotland and Ireland. One of the first things we undertook was to arrive at some definition of terms. We thought it important to try to analyse the three terms prevalent in Catholic thinking, namely: (a) Evangelism (b) Evangelization and (c) Mission. For the purpose of this book, however, I am using these words loosely. I am aware that, strictly speaking, they denote differing connotations ('evangelism' and 'evangelization' have the same roots), so here I will try briefly to analyse their meaning.

Evangelism

This is the direct proclamation of the Gospel of Jesus Christ and making his name explicit. It is a conscious effort on behalf of those who experience new life in Jesus to announce the Gospel to other individuals for their salvation. It deals directly with the process of conversion to Jesus and the Church. All of this leads us to invite others to respond to the God who loves us all, by calling them into relationship with him through Jesus by the power of the Holy Spirit.

Key words: proclamation – individuals – response.

'The Church is born of the evangelizing activity of Jesus and the 12.[4]

Process: proclamation and then acceptance.

Evangelization

This is announcing the Kingdom of God, recognizing where it is already present and bringing it more fully alive. It brings the presence of Jesus into every human situation, thereby aiming at the conversion of cultures to gospel values – making humanity new. It is a process of bringing the Kingdom to people through prayer, sharing proclamation and theological reflection. It is an ongoing process of renewal of self and others, a living, daily conversion in all strata of life.

Key words: kingdom – society – process – ongoing.

Process: formation of mature Christians – nurturing – formation of leaders.

Mission

This denotes following the command of Jesus, 'Go out into the whole world.' It is the basic work of the Church. All people are called into this work, utilizing their own charisms and gifts; it is the calling of our baptism. To minister in this way is the purpose of God's people. We are anointed at baptism for mission and we should then be appointed and sent by the Church. Mission is task-orientated. Our mandate is to build up the Kingdom of God.

'Being sent' means –
   the mission of Jesus to announce the Kingdom;

the mission of the Church – to make disciples;
my mission is to be involved in any activity which supports
the mission of the Church.

Key words: command – everyone involved – task.
Process: from being anointed at baptism to being appointed for
  action.

Some definitions of evangelism

Numerous working definitions have been put forward over the
last few years. Here are some:

(1) 'To evangelize is so to present Jesus Christ in the power of
the Holy Spirit that [people] come to put their faith in God
through Him, to accept Him as their Saviour and to serve
Him as their King in the fellowship of His Church'.[5]

(2) 'To evangelize is to spread the Good News that Jesus Christ
died for our sins and was raised from the dead according to
the Scriptures and that as the reigning Lord He now offers
the forgiveness of sins and the liberating gift of the Spirit to
all who repent and believe. Our Christian presence in the
world is indispensable to evangelism and so is that kind of
dialogue whose purpose is to listen sensitively in order to
understand. But evangelism, itself, is the proclamation of the
historical, biblical Christ as Saviour and Lord with a view to
persuading people to come to Him personally and be reconciled to God. In issuing the Gospel invitation we have no
liberty to conceal the cost of discipleship. Jesus still calls all
who would follow Him to deny themselves, take up their
cross and identify themselves with His new community. The
results of evangelism include obedience to Christ, incorpor-
ation into His Church and responsible service in the world.'[6]

(3) 'To evangelize is "To proclaim (*kerygma*) with the power
of the Spirit (Acts 1:8) the incarnate, crucified, resurrected
and living Jesus Christ (Acts 2:32) as the only Saviour (Acts

4:12) and divine Lord (Phil. 2:9–11) of all Mankind (1 Tim
2:4) and of the whole person (Eph.1:22–3) in a joyful, loving
and effective way that contributes to building the Church
(Col. 1:18–23), by making Jesus known, loved, honoured,
followed and obeyed to the ends of the earth! (Mat. 28:19).'[7]

(4) 'Evangelism is "what we do to help make the Christian
    faith, life and mission a live option to undiscipled people
    inside and outside the congregation. It is also what Jesus
    Christ does through the Church's kerygma (message),
    koinonia, (fellowship) and diakonia (service) to set people
    free. Evangelizing happens when the *receiver* turns (a) to
    Christ, (b) to the Christian message and ethic, and (c) to a
    Christian congregation and (d) to the world in love and
    mission." '[8]

So evangelization involves a change of heart, an acceptance of
Jesus into all aspects of our lives, a sharing of that Good
News and an invitation to others to share with a community of
believers. This then will have ramification in all aspects of our
day-to-day living by the power of the Holy Spirit.

Misunderstandings about evangelism
It is important to mention here what evangelism is not. Evangelism is not individualistic. Evangelism is a relationship
between a person and Jesus, but it doesn't leave us on that
basis. Evangelism must bring us into community – a bit like
pregnant women, coming together so that they can share about
their pregnancies. Evangelism is not about a system. We can
help or equip others, but not merely by using a well worked-out
system. Being evangelized means meeting Jesus in a personal
relationship, and then, of necessity, I will have my own way of
sharing that encounter with others.

    Evangelism is not simply for those who like that sort of thing;
it is for the whole Church. It cannot, therefore, be just left to
the ordained ministers or religious because they are pro-
fessionals, but neither does it exclude them. It is not something

shallow, lacking in depth. On the contrary, it contains the profound message that can give happiness, joy and liberation in a person's life. It is ongoing.

Evangelism is not healthy when its sole object is to get more people to fill the pews. Some priests and ministers would say that we have enough unevangelized people already in the pews. If a particular church is to stay in business it needs people, and so may turn itself to an outreach campaign. This will, ultimately, achieve nothing, unless individuals within the church are switched on. The only one to bring people together and sustain them in an ongoing way is '*Jesus*'. A priest said to me, recently, 'The only way to get a parish working together is to have a debt on our hands. This makes people pull together in clearing the debt.' What a false premise, because as soon as the debt is cleared they are back to square one again! Evangelism is not just about dynamic speakers or well-thought-out propaganda. The Holy Spirit must be at the centre of any evangelism in bearing witness to Jesus.

Let me concentrate a little more fully on my next point about what evangelism is not, as I feel this is a very important one for Catholics. Evangelism is not the 'social gospel' to the detriment of proclaiming the name of Jesus, in whose name we do it. We Catholics want to be saved, but sometimes not from our own sins. The great fear that many people have of Jesus is the fear that he will do what his name 'Jesus' implies, 'he who saves us from our sins'. We can be willing to be saved – and to save others – from poverty, from war, from ignorance, from disease, from economic insecurity: such salvation can leave our individual selves untouched. This is why social Christianity is so popular, why there are so many who contend that the business of Christianity is to do nothing but to help in the slum areas, develop an international conscience or agitate for national and international change. This type of faith is very comfortable because it leaves the individual conscience alone. It is even possible that some people are prompted to courageous reforms of social injustices by the very uneasiness of their own conscience; often unaware that something is wrong inside themselves they attempt to compensate for it by righting the wrong on the outside. This can also happen to people who have accumulated great wealth and try to ease their consciences by giving generously to charitable movements. It brings to my mind the first temptation of Jesus in the desert. The Devil says to Jesus, 'If you are the Son of God tell this stone to turn into a loaf' (Luke 4:4). The Devil was asking Jesus to give up the salvation of people and to concentrate upon social salvation, on the false assumption that it was hungry stomachs and not corrupted hearts that made up an unhappy civilization.

Please do not deduce from this that I am against social action. I believe that social action, in fact all action, for the Christian, grows out of the personal relationship between the individual and God. Maybe this is one reason why Catholics are more at home with the word 'evangelization' (this incorporates social action) rather than the word 'evangelism', which denotes individual challenge between ourselves and Jesus. It is not good enough to be a 'do-gooder', with a good humanistic conscience, unless it is done in and through Jesus and out of a deep love of God. I think it is fair to say that Catholics lead the way in social action both in our teaching and in practice. But social architects have found out that you cannot create a 'new' order without 'new' people and evangelists have found that abstract love cannot be preached in situations of social deprivation. The two have to home into each other. It is not a question then of either/or but of both/and.[9] The 'social' gospel is an integral element of evangelization.

Lastly, evangelism does not produce a religion that has nothing to do with sin. When I talk with non-Christians, the topic of God inevitably arises. Doing a lot of travelling I get the opportunity of meeting many people. The question will undoubtedly be asked, 'What do you do for a living?' I am always proud to witness that I am a priest. God is quickly brought into the conversation, because there is a natural curiosity in people when faith of any kind is discussed. I find that as long as I keep the conversation at the level of God then there is no problem. God can be moulded into our own image. He can be Buddha, Allah, Jehovah, and so on. Even the great movie *Star Wars* has the line, 'May the Force be with you'. But when the person of Jesus is introduced then people get uneasy because they are challenged with belief in the divinity of Jesus. They are also challenged as to why he came on earth. He was not just a good man but the second person of the Trinity who brought us back from sin at a great cost. Maybe Catholics, too, are reticent to use the name Jesus when we talk about God. We will call him 'Our Lord', 'Our Saviour', 'Blessed Lord', but, rarely, do we call him Jesus unless we are swearing. The world is full of people who wish to knock at the door of truth, even religion, but shy away from knocking at the door of ultimate truth, namely Jesus.

So, as you can appreciate, it isn't easy to define the term 'evangelize'.

Any partial and fragmentary definition which attempts to render the reality of evangelization in all its richness, complexity and dynamism does so only at the risk of impoverishing it and even distorting it. It is impossible to grasp the concept of evangelization unless one tries to keep in view all its essential elements.[10]

Reflections on the past

I realize that it is easy to look back through history and find fault with the actions of our ancestors. The same can be true as we reflect on the pre-Vatican II Church. My gazing back over the years is not meant to be negative but simply to find out where we came from and, therefore, to be better equipped to know what we are facing today.

I remember as a young child going to school, that Friday was 'black baby' day. I would pester my mother and father for a penny to give to the 'black babies'. This penny would go to missionaries who were evangelizing those poor black people with the message of the Church. In this book it is not relevant to look into the sociological or anthropological dimension of our Western Church's practices; it is sufficient to say that we saw evangelism then as something 'we did' in Africa, South America and the Orient. During the latter part of the nineteenth century and the early twentieth century many missionary orders were inaugurated, most of them to deal with the so-called 'missionary lands'. We were to some extent arrogant in almost condemning religions and cultures where great civilization existed long before Greece and Rome. Our objective was to baptize as quickly as possible as many 'heathens' as possible and make them Christians. Sometimes the methods employed to do this were, to say the least, suspect.

Thus, before Vatican II evangelism usually meant going overseas. In early days responsibility for this was in the hands of the Spanish and Portuguese. Later it was put into the hands of the missionary institutes. We in Europe to some extent hived off our responsibility to evangelize on to priests, nuns and missionaries. We even gave money to keep the mission-fields alive. In our desire to see others evangelized we forgot about ourselves. Vatican II and *Evangelii Nuntiandi* clearly shook us in their many exhortations towards self-evangelization. After all, we can only give away what we have assimilated and are living ourselves. In the past we assumed that, because we had enough priests and religious to carry on the work, all was well. Our priests and religious in the Western World were often not working with us; they were working instead of us. For example, a priest in Newcastle said to me, 'My people think they are okay as long as I remain faithful.' Now we have the crisis in the Western Church of a decline in vocations and, basically, we don't know how to cope. I can imagine God sitting on his throne listening to our prayers for more vocations. He is probably scratching his head saying, 'I cannot give you a new theology in which all of you must take responsibility and at the same time give you lots of vocations so that you can have an excuse for not getting involved. But I will give you enough vocations.' The Church of the Third World, that we have helped to evangelize, has had greater scope to grow in maturity than we in the Western Church. While recognizing that the Church of the Third World has still lots of problems, I believe our Church of the so-called First World is in desperate need of evangelizing.

The Irish people, to their credit, have given their share of men and women to overseas evangelizing. Irish seminaries were usually full of students preparing to minister in places like Australia, New Zealand, the USA and, particularly, in Britain. These men and women preached the Gospel fearlessly. Now that well has run dry, and there are not enough vocations even to staff Irish dioceses. Maybe Vatican II had a great influence on the lack of immigrant missionaries, because this clearly indicates that every local church must be an evangelizing church. The problem with priests going overseas was that the local church in the receiving area thought of itself as something foreign. One English priest was asked on arriving in his parish, 'What part of Ireland do you come from, Father?' He was amazed because there wasn't a drop of Celtic blood in his veins. The underlying assumption to the question was that all Catholics priests in England had to have some Irish blood in their body.[11]

So, maybe, we are beginning to realize that evangelizing is not something we do for other people. But would we admit that we now need evangelizing ourselves? Although it is true to say that Jesus Christ was sent into the whole world to bring the Good News to all peoples and to all nations, he belonged to a particular country, with its own history, religion and culture. By this he underlined how important it is for us to realize that we all have a country of our own. Whatever nationality or country, we have a particular responsibility for bringing the Good News to our own people first. Our Western situation calls for a systematic outreach, with new methods and a new language, to announce Jesus Christ again to those who are far from him. 'Today there is a very large number of baptised people who for the most part have not formally renounced their baptism but who are entirely indifferent to it and not living in accordance with it.'[12]

Reflections on the present

In many parts of the world there are 'not-yet Christians', but here in the West we have 'no-longer Christians'. When I go to parishes, cities, towns – particularly in Britain, Ireland and the USA – I am confronted with the same stories. There are people leaving the Church, sometimes to join other denominations or sects. The young are disillusioned with the Church. There are church crises and school crises. It is difficult to get people to attend anything other than Mass. The liturgy is lifeless, sermons are boring, with people wishing to get out of church as quickly as possible. Outside church circles, too, there is great discontent within Western society in general. The statistics show us that there are increases in rapes, muggings, murders and suicides, hijackings and kidnappings. Sexual crimes are soaring, together with political unrest. One has only to read the newspapers in every country and in every town and city to see the bold headlines of crimes committed. Each nation is spending more and more time and money to combat crime and delinquency, but these still increase. Just as we hope crime has reached its peak, we hear something more hideous. We are caught in the midst of all of this, and we have tried all the 'ologies' we can think of, to no avail. My contention is that the once-proud West, with all its evangelizing spirit to foreign lands, has itself now lost a sense of God. And having lost a sense of God, it has also lost a sense of sin. When a nation stops believing in God it begins to believe in itself and in every fad that comes along. Our Western society has changed a great deal since World War II. Carl Jung, a father of modern-day psychology, has written:

Through his scepticism the modern [Western] man is thrown back upon himself; his energies flow towards their source and wash to the surface those psychic contents which are at all times there but lie hidden in the silt as long as the stream flows smoothly in its course. How totally different did the world appear to medieval man!

For him the earth was eternally fixed and at rest in the centre of the universe, encircled by the course of the sun that solicitiously bestowed its warmth. Men were all children of God under the loving care of the Most High who prepared them for eternal blessedness and all knew exactly what they should do and how they should conduct themselves in order to rise from the corruptible world to an incorruptible and joyous existence. Such a life no longer seems real to us, even in our dreams.[13]

Perhaps what I have written sounds pessimistic, and I admit that it is a little one-sided, because both in the Church and in society there is much that is positive. I am simply highlighting the fact that Europe is missionary territory; we no longer have to go to the Third World to find the scope and outlet to evangelize. It is within our own community, town and city, that our light must shine to combat the darkness of a conflict-prone Europe. We cannot hide our heads in the sand like the proverbial ostrich. I see the need to evangelize as being critical (in the West in particular) to any general movement for the renewal of faith and the reversal of present downhill trends.

The condition of a conflict-aware society is very favourable ground in which to evangelize. Why? Because the Church exists to proclaim the Gospel for the sake of the world. It is her duty to know where and how and why this world is in darkness and lacking any redemptive message. To do this she must understand the needs of the day and speak into those needs, not into a vacuum. It is no good answering questions that no one is asking. But it must be said also that it is not the Church's duty to compile a dossier on the evils of the world and then add her voice to the prophets of doom.

Here I must point out a temptation we can all fall into, of thinking that a community that wants to renew itself must not engage in any evangelizing work until later. This is self-delusion: (a) because we can never be completely successful in renewing ourselves; (b) because any evangelism applied to a church that lacks mission would make that church inward-looking and, therefore, prone to heresy; and (c) the best way to be evangelized is to evangelize directly ourselves.

It can be said without exaggeration that the 'Christian West' has become a most difficult mission area. Evangelizing a 'post-Christian' people, those who don't think they need it, those who are hurt by the Church and those marginalized or alienated from her is hard ground to plough. To do it we need new courage, new zeal, new inspiration, and above all a new vision – if hopelessness sets into our hearts we are defeated. There is no room for complacency in European Catholicity. The fact that the Church's past goes back 2,000 years is no indicator that we have a golden right to another 2,000.

A few years ago I was privileged to be in Turkey. I walked around the streets, especially in the area of Ephesus. I was very much aware that St Paul preached powerfully in that region. He even formed a very vibrant Christian community there. Yet today it is non-existent. I'm aware that we, as Catholics, often say that 'the Holy Spirit' is with the Church. I know that he is, but the Holy Spirit may well desert us if we do not co-operate as effective builders of the Kingdom in reconstructing the Catholic Church. Shortly after the Holy Spirit touched my life in a deeper way, I was posed with the question, 'Do I stay here in Europe or do I go to the Third World where Christianity is flourishing?' I want to be where God is doing something – I do not want to minister to a dying Church. I saw and I see great signs of hope. People cannot *live* without hope; they merely exist. But there will always be great signs of hope when we take seriously the command of Jesus, 'Go out to the whole world' (Mark 16:15).

On the other hand, the Church down through the ages has been tempted to continue her existence by human means. She depended on councils, financial security and political power. This usually turned her into a human establishment erring on the side of the wealthy and often corrupt governments. Many of our people, especially the young, are rejecting our earthly powerful Church. We are endeavouring to shake off the trappings of earthly power so that our Church can have a truly prophetic voice in the midst of all the decadence. The call of St Paul must always be heard, 'How many of you were wise in the ordinary sense of the word, how many were influential people, or came from noble families? No it is to shame the wise that God chose what is foolish by human reckoning' (1 Cor. 1:26–7). The advice which the Church has to give to the world is *hope* in Jesus.

The future

One of the great reasons for hope, as I see it, is the large number of people who are hungry for God. Why do I say a large number when, recently, the statistics show us that Christianity in the West is on a downward trend. Firstly, because in my meeting with thousands of people each year – both church and unchurched – I have found very few who have made up their minds as professed atheists. Secondly, from the findings of our own mission team who knock on approximately 8000 doors each year, 90 per cent of the homes are open to listen, and prayer is very rarely, if ever, refused. Thirdly, I believe that people are made in the image and likeness of God's own Son, Jesus, and their hearts do not settle until they settle in God. As St Paul puts it, 'Blessed be God the Father of Our Lord Jesus, who has blessed us with all the spiritual blessings of heaven in Christ. Before the world was made he chose us, chose us in Christ . . . and to live . . . in his presence' (Eph,

1:3–4). Our task then is to put the Spirit of God in touch with people's spirits, 'The Spirit himself and our spirit bear united witness that we are children of God' (Rom. 8:16).

The 'God is dead' theory of people's thinking is demonstrably not working. The Communists of this century have tried it, but Russian writers are only too quick to point out that they believe Russian Christianity will give a new direction to the West. To try and push God out is nonsense because he is the 'Hound of Heaven' who will constantly be in search of his people. The stories in the Bible are but a catalogue of events with God in pursuit of sinful humanity. Half the people find it difficult to believe in God because of popular pressure from the sceptical age in which we live, and the other half is searching for a spiritual reality. We live, however, in an age where the popular image of the Church is one of irrelevancy and marked by a lack of vitality. So often our Catholic Church is not producing an alternative to worldly values. This, however, does not negate the spiritual search that continues inside people. That is why anything to do with Jesus is big box-office news, sometimes even causing controversy (*The Last Temptation of Christ* film in 1988 being an example). Films like Zefferelli's *Jesus of Nazareth* helped to make its producers and actors rich. The success of such films would be impossible were it not for the great hunger which exists in people.

If that spiritual hunger is not filled by our preaching and witnessing to Jesus, then it will be occupied by other spiritual realities. Since the decline of belief in God there has been a rapid growth in spiritualism, witchcraft and the occult. Northern Ireland is a prime example where the growth in the occult is going hand-in-hand with the atrocities there. How crazy it is to think that in the age of fantastic scientific advancement people are turning more and more to an interest in the supernatural. Is it any wonder that the Church is recommending to its priests, especially in the sacrament of reconciliation, prayers for healing and deliverance?

In 1987, when in London one weekend I did a little survey.

I picked up the newspaper simply to find out for myself what proportion of supernatural and occult movies were being shown in the West End. To my amazement almost 60 per cent of the movies that weekend had some supernatural dimension. The following week I was in New York and the proportion there was 65 per cent. Surely this tells us something. Also, in any video shop also, large sections are occupied by occult material. The young are, obviously, the most vulnerable to all of this. When the Church stops doing her job of proclaiming the Gospel in a relevant way, we cannot be too surprised that spiritual 'kicks' are obtained through other media.

If we are going to reconstruct our Church for the future, we do indeed start from this great vantage point of God embuing people with this great longing for his Deity. So if we can employ the Holy Spirit to touch first and foremost our experiences, we can then educate and organize a convinced Church. Many people, being highly suspicious of anything experiential, have and will argue that this is no longer necessary. Nevertheless many people are truly hungry for God and are eager and open to hear the truths upon which that reconstruction can begin. Any evangelizing for the future needs to be founded on basic Christian truths which can give us solid foundations upon which to build.

Solid Foundations – The Basics

Necessity for truth

My brother Michael is a stonemason by trade. As a young boy I would sit beside him asking questions and watching him spread the plans for a new house upon the table. These plans would be drawn up before any block was laid or any trowel grasped. Michael would know exactly what that new house was going to look like by merely reading those plans. He could tell me how many windows, how many doors and, very often, how much material would be needed in its construction. I would then watch the men dig deep into the ground so that lots of concrete could be poured in and left to set. One day I asked Michael 'Why pour in so much concrete? Wouldn't a little do?' He replied, 'If we don't put enough concrete into the foundations the house may stand for a little while but, eventually, it will fall because its base isn't strong enough.'

If the answer here is so clear, is it going to be any different in building the body of Christ? Unless we have put in a solid foundation, unless we grasp the basics of Christianity, our Church will be built on sand. 'Everyone who listens to these words of mine and acts on them will be like a sensible man who built his house on rock. Rain came down, floods rose, gales blew and hurled themselves against that house and it did not fall: it was founded on rock' (Matt. 7:24–25).

In 1988, millions of people in Bangladesh were left homeless because their houses were built in precarious places. They suffered not only homelessness; disease, pestilence and death followed. The aftermath of this disaster could not be cleared up in a few days but will remain with the Bangladeshi people for decades to come. If we don't get it right to start with, we will pay the price later on.

So, too, with our faith; if we don't understand and assimilate the truths of our faith we pay dearly for it. Truth is essential. I was privileged, early in my priesthood, to minister in a grade 'A' high-security prison. It was a time of great growth for me and gave me an opportunity to come face to face with people who had committed hideous crimes. One day I was called to the prison hospital to visit a man named James. The doctor had told me that he had cancer and was due to be released on compassionate grounds. James had committed a callous murder ten years previously and was now about to meet his Maker. James and I spent a long time talking about life in general. Then he rose up in his bed and asked, 'Please, Father, tell me the truth so that I can face it head on?' It is difficult, sometimes, to know how far one can go with the truth. But he continued, 'Am I going to die?' 'Yes,' I replied. Now our conversation entered a new realm. We had time to share about God. James was released. He died shortly afterwards and I was honoured to be able to officiate at his requiem. All of this had started with a word of truth shared in love with a dying man.

I take nothing for granted now, especially with Catholics, but simply go back constantly to the beginning. I'm aware that not everything can be taught but, if evangelism is anything, then surely it must build solid foundations on which the life-long Christian life can be supported. People do like to know where they stand.

What are basics?[1]

Part of my prison ministry was at a Borstal for boys aged between 14 and 16, where I was supposed to say Mass each week. Soon I was getting disillusioned, because the Eucharist was meaningless to them. So I stopped celebrating the Eucharist and began to proclaim the Trinity and its significance. If, after six weeks, these youngsters could leave Borstal with an understanding of what the sign of the cross (crossing themselves) meant then I felt I had accomplished something. Why the sign of the cross? Because the basics of our faith are contained in the words Father – Son – Holy Spirit or, putting it another way, Creator – Redeemer – Sanctifier. Let's examine this.

The Father

When one of the first Russian cosmonauts returned from a space flight he said that he 'hadn't seen God out there'. On the other hand an American astronaut, asked if he had met God in space, answered, 'I would have done if I had stepped out of my space suit'. These are two contrasting understandings of the word God.[2]

Yet the Bible states, 'Ever since God created the world, his everlasting power and deity . . . have been there for the mind to see in the things he has made' (Rom 1:20). So those people who look at the universe cannot talk themselves out of the creativeness of God the Father.

If we assent to this as the most basic element in our faith, then our God is a deity of tremendous power. But are we, or the world, the highest form of creation? The Bible indicates that angels are the highest form of creation (Col. 1:15–18). This whole appreciation of angels meets with scepticism in our modern day. 'Surely', one academic said to me, 'you don't believe in that sort of thing. It's the 1990s.' Yet some of the great saints and theologians, for example, deal at length with the topic of angels.[3] There is a great danger in present times that the affirmation about angels will be rejected as myth. The Devil, who is understood to be the prince of angels, 'is not to be regarded as a mere mythological personification of evil in the world; the existence of the Devil cannot be denied. We must, therefore, apply to the Devil whatever theology has to say about evil and sin'.[4] I tried at length, on an academic level, to come to terms with the whole problem of evil. I read many of the great philosophies but, apart from whetting my appetite for knowledge, none of them adequately answered my questions. The understanding of the Bible and the teachings of Christianity are more logical, reasonable and palatable.

When an explanation and defence of the Church's teaching about the Devil is required . . . people, today, must first have their attention drawn to the sinister superhuman power of evil in history. This has its grounds in the doctrine of the 'Principalities and Powers', and this prevents it being glossed over and reduced to triviality.[5]

There is opposition between God and the Devil, and this reached its culmination in Jesus' life as he moved towards his passion (Luke 22:3–31; John 13:27). It is sufficient to say in truth that there is a Devil and he is extremely active in modern-day society – why else would bishops create more and more official exorcists for that particular ministry? (The Diocese of Milan created forty exorcists in 1986.) It was not the Father who created evil but the Prince of the Angels, who with his adherents fell away from God and was thrust out of heaven (Rev. 12:7–12). There was a time when not to believe in the Devil and Hell was absolute heresy, but now the opposite is true and the clergy fall over backwards to redefine Satan to make him more congenial to modern taste.[6] Vatican II says that we are freed by the Son of God from the Devil's domination. The 'Evil One' led people astray into sin but his power was broken by Christ's death and resurrection.[7]

Let me introduce a story,

God created the heavens and the earth. He created everything through the use of words, for words, of course, are power. 'Let it be done,' God proclaimed, and it was done, And everything He made was good.

Well God was especially proud and loving of the man and woman He had made because He had breathed into them a part of Himself, His Spirit. But the Devil, not surprisingly, was jealous and very angry. He sauntered up one day as God was enjoying the man and the woman in the garden. He asked what God liked so much about these creatures. When God opened His mouth to speak, the Devil craftily bound His tongue. God could not talk.

The Devil then laughed at God and quietly had his way with the man and woman. As eons went by the Devil came back to mock God – he couldn't resist, such is his nature. He scoffed at the silent deity and God responded by holding up one finger. 'One,' asked the Devil, 'are you trying to tell me you just want to say one word?' 'Yes', God nodded pleading with His soft eyes. The confident Devil thought to himself, 'Not even God could do much harm with one word'. So the Devil removed the bond from God's tongue. And God spoke one word in a whisper. He spoke it for the man and woman and it brought great joy. It was a word that gathered up all the love and forgiveness and creativity God had been storing up in His heart during the time of His silence. The word He spoke was JESUS.[8]

The power of the word of God (cf. John 1), in my story, confirms the necessity of proclamation in any evangelization process.

Even the finest witness will prove ineffective in the long run if it is not explained, justified . . . There is no true evangelization if the name, teaching, the life, the promises, the Kingdom, and the mystery of Jesus of Nazareth, the Son of God are not proclaimed.[9]

Why Jesus?

Let me return to the story above. God our Father created people and endowed them with free will. They could choose

God or themselves. Through the temptation of the Devil they chose themselves. That is what we call 'original sin'. In choosing themselves a rift developed between God and humanity; only Jesus could bridge it.

So it is because of our alienation – fallen nature if you like – that God was faithful to his promise. Jesus is the bridge. Most people would grant that there is some primordial tendency to evil (sin) in the collective unconsciousness which influences all members of the human race. This is original sin at work. Most parents, for example, will say that their young child will learn to say 'no' before it says 'yes'. Even from birth we have a disposition towards selfishness and self-centredness rather than towards obedience. What is the underlying cause of all of this? We can eliminate the antiquated idea that poverty or social deprivation is the cause of inner disharmony – if that were so all the rich would be 'normal'. (Sometimes there is more abnormality among the rich and famous than among the poor.) Nor is the cause to be found in our animal background; the fact that people can laugh, create things, and such like, indicates that people are 'higher' than animals. The cause of conflict cannot be the environment, because a golden bit does not make a better horse. Judas is a good example of this; tradition has it that he came from a prosperous home. Inner disposition to evil and sin does not come from ignorance; if it did, all the academic world would be saints.

But it has to be said that people are neither totally corrupt nor totally good. We have aspirations to do good but somehow find it impossible. I suppose our predicament can be likened to that of an orchestra or music group. If one of its members plays a 'bum' note it will, invariably, affect the whole sequence. The leader of the band can stop the music and start again, but he certainly cannot deny that it has happened. The discord, certainly, will not correct itself. Can our discord be stopped? Not by people, but only by an intervention on the part of God, namely Jesus. The original discord (sin) could not be stopped by the person who committed it. Adam and Eve contracted a debt which they could not pay. The debt could only be paid by the Divine Musician. God could seize the note but not the musicians because he had already made them free.

God wanted to create a new symphony so he prepared an orchestra (the Jewish people) and a new band-leader (Mary) from whom the genius of an impressario would be born. Since it was a woman who played a key part in starting the first discordant note, a woman would be given the chance to put it right. A fallen angel tempted the first woman, now an unfallen angel (Gabriel) would consult with the new Eve. This angel would ask Mary, 'Will you be the mother of the new Adam (Jesus)?' Being born of a woman he will be a man. Being born of a virgin he will be sinless. Catholics hold Mary in high esteem because it was she who was given the greatest charter of freedom, to which she answered 'Yes'.

Recently, I stood by an English canal. The water below the lock-gate was dirty while the area above it was clean. There was a nice clean boat in dirty water making its way into the clean area. I thought to myself that this picture is very much like our lives. The dirty water is our fallen nature, the boat is Jesus, the lock gate is Mary opening herself up to allow Jesus to pass through to the clean upper area. We have to get on that boat in order to move from a state of murkiness into a state of cleanliness – but we have a choice.

For the most part we believe, as Catholics, that we can cross this boundary by our own efforts. We cannot; we need to get into the boat of Jesus. We cannot pull ourselves up to God or to a state of cleanliness by our own boot-strings. There can be no crossing from one side of the lock to the other but by way of the cross.

God shared the agony of Calvary; that is the measure of God's love. But it doesn't finish there. The boat passes through the lock gate from the dirty water into the clean water of resurrection. When we travel on that boat it doesn't cost us a penny. The fare of love is not deserved and cannot be earned. The expense is covered by the owner of the boat. There is simply no charge. This free gift is salvation in Jesus Christ the Son of God. This is what we call GRACE; this is the Good News. We are exonerated in the power of the cross.

The cross is central

Redemption

In our faith we tend to use big words, religious words, which I believe people are familiar with but do not, necessarily, understand. One of these words is 'redemption'. We are redeemed by the cross of Jesus. The meaning of the word 'redemption' is to 'be set free by the payment of a price. The ransom, therefore, is paid as a substitute for the person held in captivity.'[10] Sin, both original and our own, explains the necessity for redemption. Jesus came to release you and me from this sin and regain for us the love of the Father. Adam lost that light and strength for posterity, now the new Adam (Jesus) restores it. Satan is still permitted to tempt us but his stronghold over the human race has been broken by the strength of the cross. St Peter puts it like this: 'Remember the ransom that was paid to free you . . . not in anything corruptive, neither in silver nor gold, but in the precious blood of a lamb . . . namely Christ' (1 Pet. 1:18–20).

The cross and redemption of Jesus is something objective. Today people can say, 'Well, if that makes you happy, okay.' The truth is that Jesus freed all men and women, and made it possible for all of us to participate in that freedom. Basic truths like these need to be reiterated in every age, especially in our age. The Church affirms this truth by saying:

> As an innocent lamb, Christ merited for us life by the free shedding of His own blood. In Him God reconciled us to Himself and among ourselves; from bondage to the Devil and sin. He delivered us so that each one of us can say with the Apostle, 'The Son of God loved me and gave Himself up for me.' (Gal. 2:20)[11]

Jesus took upon himself what was due to us. Here is the para-
dox. This tremendous discovery of ours which should make us
remorseful and drive us to despair, instead fills us with joy and
hope. To emphasize what I mean let me narrate this story
which will serve to impress upon us the reality of the cross:

> After World War II ended a French resistant fighter used to
> visit a British soldier's grave each year. One day a villager
> asked him, 'Is that your son?' 'No,' replied the man, 'when
> fighting broke out during the Allied push through France, I
> was supposed to go and fight, but I had six children and my
> wife was sick. I knew my family couldn't survive without me,
> so I met this British boy who said that he would go in my
> place. A short time afterwards he was wounded and was
> brought to a hospital not far from here where he died later.
> This is his grave and this is the inscription I wanted to carve
> on his tombstone . . . "He died for me".'

We can see that this was an instance of heroic mercy. But there
is an even greater one. Each one of us can say the same thing
as that man: 'He (Jesus) died for me.' Christ took *my* place
and died instead of *me*, so that I have the potential to live. So
I am free from the power of sin, free from guilt; I am free to
be a child of God.

Reconciliation
Another of those words which is very much misunderstood
by Catholics is 'Reconciliation'. We see it sometimes as just
confessing our sins to a priest. While not excluding this, reconciliation goes much further and is closely linked to Jesus and
the cross. Reconciliation is about being restored back into a
loving relationship. The area that causes people most concern
in our generation is that of relationships. How can we possibly
understand a true relationship when the majority of our
relationships are so mixed up. In my ministry as a priest I have
found that the whole area of relationships 'screw' people up.
It's not really surprising, because we are being bombarded

with flippant relationships on the media all the time. True relationships are not held up as examples on our TV screens. Instead, the media and the newspapers highlight wrong and – yes, I will use the word – sinful relationships. Our young are growing up to think that these relationships are the norm. If there is one area that the Devil attacks vehemently it is the area of relationships. He has only to put his finger on two raw areas, and he has the whole of society. He attacks, first, the area of relationships in marriage, causing strain, tension, depression, rows, alienation and, eventually, separation or divorce. The knock-on effects are colossal, both emotionally and financially. He, in fact, breaks up the whole fabric of stable society. The second area he attacks is the area of commitment in celibacy. This breaks up priestly and religious commitment. The prophetic power of gospel living is diminished and the Gospel can no longer be preached by these people authentically. Erroneous relations are no respecters of persons or professional classes.

The essence of original sin is, basically, a broken relationship between us and God. We cannot live in broken relationships – they tear us apart – so there was an urgent need for reconciliation between God and humanity. St Paul puts it like this: 'But God loved us with so much love that he was generous with his mercy . . . and gave us a place with him in heaven, in Christ Jesus' (Eph.2:4–6).

Since the cross removed the barrier of alienation, we are no longer estranged but reconciled and are acceptable in the presence of God. We were once at one with God, then aliens through our own fault, but now integrated again into that loving relationship. The cross is the bridge between a sinful people and a Holy God.

Justified

The last of the three words to be dealt with here is 'justified'. To illustrate what I mean, here is another story. I was making my way along Route 75 towards Fort Myers in Florida in 1987.

I was thinking about this word and finding it difficult to explain it to people. Then a picture came into my mind. I was standing in a Law Court before three magistrates. The Clerk of the Court was reading out all my faults. I had to admit in my picture that I was guilty of all these things. When the clerk had finished the three judges collaborated for a moment and I felt sure that sentence was going to be pronounced. The verdict was 'Not guilty'. The court scene in my picture was that of Heaven. I was standing before the Throne of God, not a human court where punishment would have been pronounced. When I was prepared to confess 'Guilty' to all my sins, the verdict of 'Not guilty' was returned by the Triune God because of the cross of Jesus. Acquittal is the verdict because of the victory won by the cross. The term 'justified' is taken from the courts of law. A person is set free from this court without a penny to pay, and when we are acquitted once we cannot be tried again for the same crime. Since Jesus, who was innocent of our crime, has paid the debt for our guilt we walk out of the court of judgement totally freed.

This is the truth of the Gospel. The principal article of our faith, as Christians, is that through the cross of Jesus Christ we are redeemed, reconciled and justified. To be evangelized, in the words of the Church, means, 'that in Jesus Christ, the Son of God made man, who died and rose from the dead, salvation is offered to all men [people] as a gift of God's grace and mercy'.[12]

So Jesus, while still a man, was clearly something more. Jesus belongs to our world and he belongs to God's world. The human and the Divine meet again in an authentic relationship.

The Holy Spirit

It is not too difficult for us humans to cope with the terms 'Father' and 'Son.' The very words arouse acknowledgement within us. We all have a father and we are all either sons or daughters. But to understand the term 'Holy Spirit' is much more difficult. It is nebulous. We can all say, lightly, that the Holy Spirit is the third person of the Trinity. We can state an objective fact, but in doing so we limit the Holy Spirit to a doctrine of faith. Putting it simply, the Holy Spirit for most of us was the displaced person in the Trinity, tagged on at the end of the Father and the Son. Yet St Augustine wrote:

> Their [the Father's and the Son's] common Spirit, what does this mean? Is it their unity with each other, their holiness, their love? Their substantial and eternal communion? Their friendship and fellowship . . . ? Yes we can say it is their mutual charity, the love of the Father for the Son and the Son for the Father.[13]

Here is part of a letter I received sometime ago.

> Before personal conversion to Jesus, which came about in my early forties, my faith, like many others, was based on a churchgoing religion which eventually became stale and ended up as a non-churchgoing religion. In those days the Holy Spirit was an unknown quantity. He appeared in Church liturgies and ancient hymns as 'the Holy Ghost' and was an 'it' rather than a person. I suppose, if anything, I regarded him as an archaic irrelevance tied up with the musty smelling interiors of country parish churches whilst I didn't seem to recall him as ever coming to the fore in any of the churches that I attended as a youth.

The Holy Spirit is a living manifestation of the love between the Father and the Son. Yet the Holy Spirit is also the living experience whereby God communicates himself to us humans. I have written at length about the Father and Jesus; we can see how they fit into our world picture. Where does the Holy Spirit fit in? To answer this question I look at the lives of the disciples. I always felt that when they walked the earth with Jesus they would have been convinced about who he was. They stood by him when he healed the sick, raised the dead, cast out devils. Surely they must have believed that he was God.

But we find instances, like the calming of the storm, when they turned to each other and asked, 'Who can this man be?' They were convinced of his godliness, but were they convinced that he was God? He kept saying to them that they wouldn't understand fully what he was all about until they received the Holy Spirit. So these disciples basically needed to be converted to Jesus and his work. It was not possible for them to attain this by their own strength, only by the power of the Holy Spirit. We, too, are in the same situation; we can know all about Jesus but not really know Jesus. We need to be evangelized, and the power which evangelizes us is the power of the Holy Spirit. We need conversion.

So the Holy Spirit is fundamental because:

(1) He will show the world how wrong it was about sin (John 16:8). Through their recognition of sin people can enter into the life of Jesus.

(2) He will feed and build up the Church. The Church is the fellowship of the Holy Spirit in which those who may not share a lot in common, in secular terms, are drawn together by the Holy Spirit. This work of the Holy Spirit is not selfish in nature, but in turn sends us out in concern for other.

(3) The Holy Spirit brings us to faith in Jesus. The Church is made up of individuals who need to be constantly built up in the workings of the Spirit. Previously dead to the message of Jesus we are enlivened and quickened to new life by the power of the Spirit. In this power we are able to confess 'Jesus is Lord' (1 Cor.12:3).

(4) The Holy Spirit sustains and develops each individual in Christ. We cannot attain to salvation by our own efforts or deeds but only by the touch of the Holy Spirit.

Be converted anew

When churchgoing people find out that I am a Catholic evangelist they inevitably point me in the direction of those in their church who are 'lapsed', they don't seem to see any need for those in the pews to be constantly converted. The messages of recent popes indicate that church people do need to hear the message afresh and be asked to respond to it. So, what do I mean by 'allowing the Holy Spirit to convert us anew'. If it is a divine power (the Holy Spirit), do I simply wait for it, like lightning from heaven? Is it a matter of temperament? Is there a human element involved? Here are some pointers toward answering these questions.

First, as human people, we must turn to God. We must be willing to turn away from sin, and indeed any bondage, in order that God can meet us half-way. There can be no half-measure in this process; we cannot bargain with God nor can we keep a foot in each camp. God clearly states that we are either for him or against him (Rev. 3:16). We need to be willing to turn towards God. This is what I mean by repentance.

Secondly, as we have seen earlier, we must believe that Jesus has mastered sin, death and evil and that he has the ability to master these things also in our lives. He can put a clean heart and a new spirit in us.

Thirdly, many of you reading this book were probably baptized as infants. There is, sometimes, an idea among us that baptism is some sort of magical rite which will of itself admit us to a relationship with God. While this is true, it does need our own personal 'yes' to what happened to us all those years ago. Our personal 'yes' to our own baptism is part of conversion and, therefore, part of Christian initiation. Baptism, of its essence, means a dying to the 'old self' so that a new person can emerge.

Fourthly, we must be open to be filled with the Holy Spirit or, putting it another way, filled with the power of God. We must put to rest the old idea that we are not holy enough, or that it only happens to special people, or that it will happen near death, or that it can never really be achieved. To be filled with the Spirit is part of conversion, an essential part, so that we can live out what we believe on a day-to-day basis. The neglect of 'being filled with the Holy Spirit' may account for so many ineffective Catholics in our churches.

The fifth, and probably the most contentious element in the process of conversion, is membership of a church. To say that we belong to the Church is too vague. We must, in practice, be committed to a body of people. So there are some 'freelance' Catholics who wander from church to church but are committed to none. There are others who suggest that one can believe in Jesus without going to church at all. Also we have in our churches some few 'church-hoppers', who belong to a particular geographic parish but don't worship in the church there; they attend Mass in another church, but refrain from getting involved anywhere. Maybe we clergy have ourselves to blame slightly for this problem because, in the past, we asked little of our people except to turn up for Mass. Now we are asking for commitment to a particular church. I am not suggesting that each person must go to his or her geographic parish, but they should not 'cop out' and evade their calling or involvement in the church they do attend. Our conversion needs to be lived out in a practical way with others. When we do become committed to a particular body or church, we are then *accountable* for our actions. God means to deliver us from individualism and into community (church). People can only have their faith built up and obtain teaching for growth when they live within a body of Christians. We need a structure in which to function, otherwise there is chaos.

The Holy Spirit's function, then, is to make all of these real. It is not something vague, obscure or impractical. All the above five elements are involved in becoming *fully* converted to Jesus. So let me ask you the question, 'Have you been fully converted?' None of the above are optional extras, and many problems arise when we see only one or two of them as necessary and sufficient.

To evangelize 'will never be possible without the action of the Holy Spirit . . . It is in the "consolation of the Holy Spirit" that the Church increases. The Holy Spirit is the soul of the Church.'[14]

The Kingdom

The last basic concept that I want to deal with in this chapter is 'the Kingdom'. I know it is a multi-faced concept which demands some interpretation. The Kingdom of God has been held up for a long time as the proverbial carrot. If we live a good life then we will be given this prize as our reward. We rarely thought of the Kingdom as something now. We are called to live in the present Kingdom so that the future glory is merely a passing into completeness of that Kingdom. I don't have to wait until I die to experience the Kingdom of God.

'The Kingdom and this salvation, which are the key words of Jesus Christ's evangelization, are available to every human being as grace and mercy.'[15] By the power of the Holy Spirit we can enter into a new understanding of what it means to be a citizen of God's Kingdom. But it is no joy-ride. Sometimes the Kingdom is portrayed as a luxury-liner going for a Mediterranean cruise. Apart from being inaccurate, this understanding is positively harmful. The Kingdom is best described as a battle-weary hulk in deep water with the assurance of Jesus that it won't sink (Matt. 28:20). It is a costly kingdom. 'If anyone wants to be a follower of mine . . . let him take up his cross daily and follow me' (Mark 8:34).

First, the Kingdom of God is a kingdom in this world peopled by everyone, yet understood, professed and lived by those who clearly say 'yes' to the King (Jesus). As citizens of this Kingdom we will constantly be in opposition to ourselves (weakness, selfishness), to the world around us and to the Devil. We are in conflict with ourselves, constantly, in the tug-of-war which exists within us. We hear the voice of God, asking us to be faithful, while our own weaker selves pull in the other direction. St Paul puts it like this:

I cannot understand my own behaviour. I fail to carry out the things I want to do, and I find myself doing the very things I hate . . . Who will rescue me from this body doomed to death? Thanks be to God through Jesus Christ our Lord! (Rom.7:15, 24–5)

The enemy loves to exploit us through temptations but God through Jesus gives us the grace to resist.

Secondly, we need to be of service to the Kingdom of God and not the Kingdom of the World. We can see in our world three main areas of delight which it presents to us, namely: power, sex and money. These will glisten in front of our eyes to seduce us into a belief that they have substance and value. Yet they are all so short-lived. Power lasts only as long as we have the upper-hand; then a stronger person arrives and dispossesses us. Sex is really a fleeting pleasure. Money builds us barns of plenty, but there are no pockets in shrouds. The Kingdom of the World blinds us into false security. The fellowship of godly citizens is our primary defence against being occupied by the Kingdom's of the World.

Thirdly, the Kingdom of Satan (the Devil) tries constantly to dispossess us from our proper inheritance. He has many names, the Destroyer, Deceiver, Liar. The Kingdom of Satan was and is the enemy of God's Kingdom. Jesus has won the victory, and we can co-operate in that victory by prayer and fasting. The Devil might win a few skirmishes but he cannot win the war. God is on the side of people, not to trick us, but to empower us.

Only the Kingdom, therefore, is absolute, and it makes everything else relative. The Lord will delight in describing in many ways the happiness of belonging to the Kingdom . . . which is liberation from everything that oppresses man but which is above all liberation from Sin and the Evil One.[16]

The way in which the Kingdom of God and its kernel 'salvation', is experienced is 'in a radical conversion, a profound change of mind and heart'.[17]

Any proclamation or teaching which excludes these basic elements of our faith will produce faulty or, at best, weak Christians. Everything must grow from these seeds; they are fundamental. Unless they have been heard, accepted and acted upon, all else will be futile: sacraments will become empty obligatory rituals; teaching will fall on deaf ears; prophecy will fail to rouse; the liturgy, especially Mass, will be spiritless; sermons will find no home; the lamp of prayer will be extinguished; and theology will become a rational or historic exercise.

This fundamental and profound exercise of asserting the basics has priority for us over everything else. It will permeate all else. In a sense all we do will be an extension of the basics into various aspects of Christian life and development. Born of the Scriptures, the teaching of Jesus and tradition, no ministry in the Church can lose touch with the freshness and vitality of these basics.

3

Building on Rock

In dealing with the whole area of conversion and 'good news', I am convinced that we must begin with the study of the biblical concepts. I am aware that the Bible cannot be studied in isolation from today's issues, but we need a starting point that provides us with a foundation on which we can examine the whole area of conversion and 'good news' throughout Christian history. Christian faith, if it is worth its salt, must involve some form of conversion. It involves personal commitment. Starting from the biblical witness we can say that conversion has to do with personal response. While the term 'to evangelize' is concerned with presenting the Good News, conversion is about our response. God calls people into community with him. From the earliest time, in the perspective of the doctrine on conversion, it has been known that the bond of community with God could be broken through the fault of people, whether it were a question of collective sins or individual sins.

Conversion in the Old Testament[1]

Most scholars would agree that the deepest roots of conversion in the Old Testament hinge around the word *shubh*. The broad meaning of the word is to 'return' or 'turn back'. *Shubh* means to return to the already existing covenant with God. This covenant was the one made by the Father with Israel: 'I will be your God if you will be my people.' The word *shubh* belongs to an already existing relationship and hence it is rarely applied to people outside Israel. So it is the people of God who are asked to return, not the pagans. This very often implies a change of conduct or a new orientation of the whole person.

The predominant use of the word *shubh* lies in the obedience of God's people to their relationship with God. The constant call to 'return' is spoken time after time because the relationship (like all relationships) was not something static but a constant response to God as he did new things with his people.

The chosen people, both individually and collectively, were constantly violating the covenant. God would have had every right to abandon them, yet he called them to conversion. The call to conversion was an essential part of prophetic preaching.

> The prophet Jeremiah proclaimed it [conversion] before all the people of Judah and all the citizens of Jerusalem . . . 'Furthermore, Yahweh has persistently sent you all his servants, the prophets, but you have not listened or paid attention. The message was this, "Turn back, each of you, from your evil behaviour and your evil actions, and you will stay on the soil Yahweh gave to you".'(Jer.25:2,4–5)

So the most expressive use of the word *shubh* is found in the prophetic writings. Amos, the prophet of justice, was not content merely to ask the people to 'seek God' in a pious context; rather he called on them to reject evil and to love good (Amos 5:14ff). He asked the people to correct their unjust conduct so that they would not incur the wrath of God. Hosea demanded that people return from idolatry to God, so that God's anger would not cloud them (Hos.14:2–9). Conversion is, therefore, related to the fact that God will judge his people. Surely this understanding of judgement is relevant today. Over the last few years we have constantly heard of the 'God of love', and rightly so. But the God of love is no Father Christmas dealing out favours willy-nilly; he is also a God of justice who will call us to account. In the Old Testament context it was only after this judgement that the return became reality.

The prophet Isaiah denounced every kind of sin – sins of justice, sins of worship, sins of politics. He declared that only

conversion could bring true blessings, for worship is meaningless unless there is true submission to God's will: 'Take your
wrong-doing out of my sight, cease to do evil. Learn to do
good, search for justice, help the oppressed, be just to the
orphan, plead for the widow' (Isa.1:16–17). Isaiah knew that
his words would run up against the hardness of the people's
hearts (Isa.6:9–10), and indeed catastrophe ensued. Isaiah's
only wish was that a few would remain faithful; only those who
were converted were to be saved (Isa.10:21). This reference to
the faithful ones is paralleled in Jeremiah; here the call is for
a renewed relationship with God after the period of exile. A
new theme is brought to bear upon the issue of conversion,
namely that of being prepared for the future. It was only in
the context of conversion that this 'remnant' would be equipped
to face the vision that God had for them. Surely this makes
sense for us today, because it is only those who have experienced a new conversion who will be able to discern and
implement in direct action the call to evangelize: 'Go out to
the whole world' (Mark 16:16).

But the collective call to 'turn back' was not made just to
the people in general; it also had a personal and individualistic
dimension. Ezekiel put it like this:

> Whenever you hear a word from me [God], warn them in
> my Name. If I say to a wicked man: You are to die, and you
> do not warn him; if you do not speak and warn him to
> renounce his evil ways and so live, then he shall die for his
> sin, but I will hold you responsible for his death.
> (Ezek.3:17–18)

So Yahweh insists on the personal character of conversion.
Each person must answer for themselves, and each will receive
the appropriate reward for their conduct (Ezek.3:10–20). It is
made clear in the Old Testament that what counts most in
personal conversion is the inner attitude, the heart, although
it is hidden from view. The 'heart', in the Hebrew mind, is
symbolic of the whole inner person, not merely the physiologi-

cal 'heart'. So gradually Israel found that external actions were not enough; to find God one had to seek him with all one's heart (Deut.4:29). What individuals in the Old Testament, as well as others down through the centuries, found was that it was not a new beginning they needed but rather a new conversion to help them begin. It takes the Creator to give that new beginning. God, himself, promised to achieve what he required of his people. 'I shall pour clean water over you and you will be cleansed . . . I shall give you a new heart and put a new spirit in you' (Ezek.36:25–6). With this new heart they recognized and regretted their evil conduct. So their knowledge of conversion was closely linked to an understanding of sin.

We can deduce from this that conversion was central to the mind of the Old Testament people. The Jewish people had been chosen to be God's people and they were constantly challenged to 'return' to their rightful role. The call to return was not just a call to the need of the hour but a response to the mighty works of God among peoples. 'Returning' was not an attempt at appeasement but God's offer of new things. The call to 'return' did not exclude the personal, but even the 'I' of the psalmist has to be seen as representing the collective nation of the covenant. On the other hand, the collective call to the nation had to be answered by the individual response to conversion. In the end, conversion always had a social dimension. It had the vertical dimension between the individual and God, but also the horizontal response – namely, it spoke to people in their day-to-day dealings. Jesus began his preaching by quoting a passage which, for me, sums up the whole message of conversion in the Old Testament:

The Spirit of the Lord has been given to me, for Yahweh has anointed me. He has sent me to bring good news to the poor, to bind up hearts that are broken; to proclaim liberty to captives, freedom to those in prison; to proclaim a year of favour from Yahweh, a day of vengeance for our God. (Isa.61:1–2; cf. Luke 4:18–19)

Conversion in the New Testament [2]

Jesus calls for conversion

The message of conversion in the Old Testament is continued very emphatically into the New Testament. It is found in the prophetic preaching and teaching of John the Baptist. John's mission is summed up by St Luke in these words:

> He will bring back many of the sons of Israel to the Lord their God. With the spirit and power of Elijah, he will go before him [Jesus] to turn the hearts of fathers towards their children and the disobedient back to the wisdom that the virtuous have. (Luke 1:16–18)

Here again the main theme is that of the acknowledgement of sin and the need to adopt a new way of living. John gave his baptism of water which was to be followed by the baptism of fire at the hands of Jesus (Matt.3:11).

Jesus, as we saw in chapter 2, came to initiate the Kingdom, but again the central message of the Kingdom was to be conversion: 'I have not come to call the virtuous, but sinners to repentance' (Luke 5:32). But the message of conversion was again to collide with selfishness and attachment to many things, especially greed and riches (Mark 10:21–5), institutionalism (Luke 18:9) and the hardness of society's heart (Matt.13:15; Isa.6:10). I will deal with these later in chapter 6.

When Jesus called for conversion he did not want mere external signs or show. What really counted for him was the inner disposition of the person, the heart: 'Why do you call me, "Lord, Lord," and not do what I say?' (Luke 6:46).

The word *shubh*, that is used so often in the Old Testament, is taken up strongly in the New Testament by the words *epistrephein* and *metanoein*. *Epistrephein* means the literal physical turning of a person, while *metanoein* means to change one's mind or being. *Epistrephein* is found mainly in the Acts of the Apostles and deals almost exclusively with 'mass conversion'; it is rarely used for the conversion of individuals. Repentance or *metanoein*, on the other hand, is almost synonymous with the preaching of Jesus and his call to 'repent'. If we are to remain true to the total New Testament understanding of conversion, then we have to bring in words like 'faith', 'justification' and 'election'.[3] Baptism and *metanoein* are closely linked in the writings of St Paul.

Conversion could mean different things depending on whether a person was a Jew or a pagan. What was basically required of a Jew in conversion was that they recognize Jesus as Lord. To this conversion (*metanoein*) God would respond by forgiving them their sins. The forgiveness of these sins would be seen in terms of baptism, and then they would receive the gift of the Holy Spirit. 'Every one of you must be baptised in the name of Jesus Christ for the forgiveness of your sins, and you will receive the gift of the Holy Spirit' (Acts 2:38). So the Jews were asked to make a positive act of faith in Jesus, and then they would return (*epistrephein*) to the Lord (Acts 3:20). But we know that the Jews had a veil over their faces. If they were to be converted then that veil would be taken away: '. . . the veil is over their minds. It will not be removed until they turn to the Lord' (2 Cor.3:15–16). Maybe there is a parallel here between the Jews and some of our so-called Christians today. Maybe, like the Jews, some of us think that we have already arrived and are in no need of conversion.

The message of conversion was more welcomed among the pagans; it was successfully preached at places like Antioch, Ephesus, Thessalonica and elsewhere. The conversion of the pagans became the special mission of St. Paul. For the pagans, however, conversion (*metanoein*) demanded that they detach themselves from idols, so that they could turn (*epistrephein*) to the real God (Acts 14:15; 26:18; 1 Thess 1:9). Once this first step of conversion (*metanoein*) is taken, all people can be led to 'come back to the shepherd and guardian of your souls' (1 Pet. 2:25).

Acts of the Apostles and conversion

The Acts of the Apostles frequently uses the terms *metanoein* and *epistrephein*, and in a way that is closely interlinked and inter-related. These words denote the very core of the missionary preaching of the early Church, in instances like Pentecost (Acts 2:38) or Peter's preaching in the temple (Acts 3:19). The whole of Paul's preaching and travelling centres around the call to conversion (Acts 26:18ff). In addition to these instances, there are five accounts of conversion experiences which I feel have important significance to us: Acts 8 (v. 26–39) gives us an account of the baptism of the Ethiopian eunuch; Acts 9 tells us about the dramatic conversion of St Paul on the road to Damascus; Acts 10 gives us a long detailed account about the conversion of Cornelius to Christianity; Acts 16 deals with the baptism of Lydia and informs us of the conversion and baptism of the jailer where Paul was in prison.

I mention these five significant accounts because in none of them are the words *metanoein* or *epistrephein* used. The conversion of St Paul is regarded as a conversion into apostleship. In fact, many of St Paul's epistles begin by stating the fact that St Paul is an apostle in his own right: 'From Paul appointed by God to be an apostle of Christ Jesus' (Col. 1:1; also Gal. 1:2; Rom. 1:1). The reason for conversion differs in each of the five cases: for instance, preaching is highlighted in the case of the eunuch and Lydia; a vision is predominant in the case of Cornelius and a miracle in the story of the jailer. Yet in all five instances conversion is closely linked to baptism which, I think, would signify some sense of visible entrance into the already existing body (church). These five instances are also closely related to the Old Testament understanding of conversion – namely, God clearly is taking the initiative himself, while the use of human instruments is relegated somewhat into the background. It is true also to point out that in each case a new stage is reached in the development of Christianity – namely, a spreading of the Gospel from Jerusalem out into the world. It is as if the divine mandate of Mark 16:16, 'Go out to the whole world,' is being accomplished very quickly. The main turning point for the early Church in the Acts was the passing of the message from the Jews to the pagans. I believe that is the reason why the story of the conversion of Cornelius is so extensive. The purpose of God is being fulfilled.

St Paul and conversion

In the writings of St Paul we have to look at another word for conversion, namely '*pisteuein*'. The meaning of this word in a missionary sense is 'to become a believer or to begin to believe'. For St Paul the work *pistis* depends on the reality of Jesus and the proclamation of his name: 'So faith comes from what is preached, and what is preached comes from the word of Christ' (Rom.10:17).[4] Conversion in this context is a direct response to the mercy of God present in the person and action of Jesus. 'It is the power of God saving all who have faith . . . since this [Jesus] is what reveals the justice of God to us' (Rom.1:16–17).

But this turning or *pistis* is related to personal decision and commitment. Those who desire God must turn of their own volition from all that holds them back from this new life. This means a turning from obstacles (chapter 6) from idols and personal securities, to become a servant of God.

In particular, I want to urge you in the name of the Lord, not to go on living the aimless kind of life that pagans live. Intellectually they are in the dark, and they are estranged from the life of God, without knowledge because they have shut their hearts to it. (Eph. 4:17–19)

The role of the Church for St Paul is the handing on of this new life (Rom.8:23). Conversion or *pistis* is the response that needs to be made by the whole of humanity. Pope Paul VI puts it like this:

There is no doubt that the effort to proclaim the Gospel to the people of today, who are buoyed up by hope but at the same time often oppressed by fear and distressed, is a service rendered to the Christian Community and also to the whole of humanity. [5]

Conversion in St John

St John also draws heavily on the Old Testament idea of conversion. It is only when God reveals himself that conversion, *pistis*, is possible. It is the light which comes into the darkness (John 1:5–10). Conversion, for St John, results in our ability to choose the light instead of the darkness. This decision is a matter for the whole world and not just for a few individuals (John 12:31; 16:8). St John is interested in terms like 'birth' and 'rebirth' (John 3:5ff), being born of God (1 John 5:4), children of God (John 1:12–20). These phrases belong the the whole context of conversion. John puts tremendous emphasis on remaining in Christ, on faithfulness to God as distinct from a once-off instance of decision (John 10:38; 17:21–6). So John is interested in a person remaining in Christ, not to the exclusion of that particular moment of conversion, but to the faithfulness of growing in holiness.

> I am the true vine and my Father is the vinedresser. Every branch in me that bears no fruit he cuts away, and every branch that does bear fruit he prunes to make it bear even more. (John 15:1–2)

A practical understanding of conversion

From all that I have written above we can see that the Bible's understanding of conversion, despite the use of differing words, is a valid and practical concept. For this reason we can see that the many efforts throughout the history of Christianity are permeated by the desire for missionary activity. We have also seen that the term 'conversion' is not a narrow fundamentalist idea but is one of great diversity. Never is conversion seen in the Old or New Testament as a purely personal experience but rather as something that affects the whole of humanity.

Nevertheless individuals have to be converted so that the whole can be transformed.

Conversion and holiness cannot be separated in the Bible. As far as the words *metanoein* and *epistrephein* (turning) are concerned, these simply *indicate the beginning of a process*. In the Old Testament conversion is a turning away from idolatry, false living and the power of evil, to be a faithful God. In the New Testament conversion is being set free, to engage or embark upon a new life in Jesus by the power of the Holy Spirit. It means to enter into discipleship with Jesus in the power of the Holy Spirit. In the New Testament conversion and holiness are closely linked to the great commission of preaching the Kingdom (Luke 24:44–9). The preaching of the Kingdom represents action: 'Go – disciple – baptize – all nations' (Matt.28:19). It is hoped by Jesus in this context that the whole cosmos will be renewed by the call to conversion and holiness of the early Church. This same call is relevant today.

Some would regard this turning, or conversion, as a once-and-forever event in the Bible. If so, it would be a non-repeatable exercise. Leon Dufour puts it differently when he writes:

> The act of conversion, sealed by baptism, was accomplished once and for always; it was impossible to renew the grace (Heb.6:6). But the baptised [converted] are capable of falling once again into sin. The Apostolic community very soon had this experience. In this case repentance is still necessary if one wishes to share in salvation in spite of everything. . . . Without speaking explicitly of the Sacrament of Penance [Reconciliation] . . . 'some texts' show that the virtue of penance must have its place in the Christian life of prolonging . . . conversion. [6]

Karl Rahner sums up, for me, the biblical understanding of conversion when he writes,

> From the biblical . . . point of view, man's free turning to

God has always to be seen as a response, made possible by God's grace, to a call from God. And he himself in the summons gives what he asks. This call of God is both Jesus Christ himself, as the presence of the Kingdom of God in person, with the demand this involves, and his Spirit which as God's self-communication offers freedom and forgiveness to overcome the narrow limits and sinfulness of man. It also comprises the actual situation of the person to whom the call is addressed. This is the precise particular embodiment of the call of Christ and the Spirit. [7]

So conversion is not an end in itself but rather a new beginning, a life of discipleship. It entails a growth in maturity and holiness, involvement in the membership of the body (Acts 2:40–7) and involvement in the world around us.

But conversion presupposes that some sort of prophetic calling has preceded it. It presupposes a preaching and listening process. There must a clear invitation for any response to be possible. Therefore the men and women of the Bible needed to have the Good News communicated to them so that they could be given a valid opportunity to turn back to God. Hence our need to look at the words 'Good News – Evangel – Gospel'. 'The nature of evangelism is to communicate the Good News; the purpose of evangelism is to give individuals or groups a valid opportunity to accept [God]; the goal of evangelism is pursuading men and women to accept Him . . . and serve Him in the fellowship of His Church.' [8]

We need a good sound biblical understanding of what the word 'Evangel' or 'Good News' or 'Gospel' means. Jesus stood up in the synagogue and read with conviction and authority at the beginning of his ministry: 'The spirit of the Lord has been given to me for he has anointed me, he has sent me to bring the good news to the poor . . .' (Luke 4:18–19). All eyes were fixed on him. It was not the young man's learning or eloquence that riveted their attention, because he was just an ordinary Jewish man. The Old Testament was well known to every one of his listeners because they were steeped in the Scriptures. What then was their understanding of the term 'Good News' and why were they so infuriated that he was appropriating this significantly poignant term to himself?

Good News in the Bible [9]

The Old Testament used the Hebrew word *basar*, which literally means the 'Good News' that salvation is at hand and is an imminent reality. It is a public announcement that something great has been worked by God. This could be a great victory, as related in 2 Samuel 18:19, 'I must run and tell the good news to the king that Yahweh has vindicated his cause by ridding him of his enemy,' or it could be a moment of deliverance, as in Psalm 98, 'Sing Yahweh a new song, for he has . . . displayed his power.' In the synagogue Jesus read from Isaiah 61. The 'good news' in this passage has a specific religious value because it announces the end of the exile for the Jewish people and the return to their homeland; it announces the coming of the Kingdom of God. This is the direct manifestation of the return of God to Sion (the Jewish nation); it proclaims the victory of God. The bearer of glad tidings is the herald who speeds on ahead of Yahweh's triumphal procession proclaiming his victory and announcing to Sion, 'Your God reigns' (Isa. 52:7). The time of salvation is actually made present by the very fact of its proclamation. This conception of the bearer of good tidings and his message of deliverance (good news) persisted as a vital reality in the history of the Jewish people. So Jesus in the New Testament becomes the herald *par excellence* and the personification of 'Good News'.

Jesus, the Good News
No doubt the Old Testament understanding of 'good news', bridged by Jesus himself, has influenced its New Testament counterpart. Nevertheless a new word is introduced to designate 'good news' namely *euangelion* or, in modern English,

'evangelism'. This word *euangelion* was probably a more secular word than *basar* and used in connection with the great events pertaining to the Roman Caesar of the day. It would have been used to highlight the birth of Caesar's heirs or to relate a great victory, but Jesus was now using it of himself, the true Saviour and the King of Caesars. So 'the time has come . . . and the Kingdom of God is close at hand' (Mark 1:15): this is the essence of the Good News.

But now the very person of the messenger becomes the centre of the Good News. He has come to tell captives that they are free, to restore sight to the blind, to liberate those who are down-trodden (Luke 4:18–19). This proclamation of the Good News is not merely idle gossip or hot air, it is going to be accompanied by the demonstration of power. Jesus was not coming to the earth to gain acclaim as a great preacher but to enter into the deep reality of people's lives. Thus, although the term 'evangelism' means to announce 'good news', Jesus was not going to separate word and action. Putting this into the context of a teaching situation, a young child will learn very little if words are the only means of communication – demonstration is also necessary to validate the points made. If we are telling a young child that one and one make two, then it is also necessary to show physically how this can be so.

The words of Good News then were not going to be empty, like those of the false prophets, but full of the evidence of truth.

Christ carried out this proclamation by innumerable signs, which amaze the crowds and at the same time draw them to him in order to see him, listen to him and allow themselves to be transformed by him: the sick are cured, water is changed into wine, bread is multiplied and dead come back of life. [10]

This bore witness to the truth. One of John's disciples asks Jesus, 'Are you the one who is to come, or must we wait for someone else?' (Luke 7:19). In answer to this question Jesus did not preach a long serman or give a drawn-out explanation, but simply said, 'Go back and tell John what you have seen . . . the blind see again, the lame walk . . . the deaf hear . . . the Good News is proclaimed' (Luke 7:22–3).

This was evangelism in action. What an extraordinary way to bring the message of evangelism to the cities of Galilee! Maybe in our churches, today, we are burdened by lots of words. People could be excused if they asked to be shown the proof of it all. These words and action of Good News were not reserved for the initiated Jews; the pagans too were disposed to listen and be recipients of the power of God (Matt. 8:5–13).

But Jesus' objective was not merely to heal bodies, but also to evoke repentance and faith. He used demonstrations of power so that people could be opened up to the challenge of the Good News. We find Jesus saying that he has not come to save the righteous but sinners. We see him eating with sinners, talking to prostitutes, calling into his service socially non-acceptable people. By his physical actions he was communicating Good News. Is it possible in our churches, today, that we are too preoccupied with the closed circles of the saved and the comfortable? Are we the keepers of an aquarium? Jesus did not proclaim Good News to institutionalize people but rather to liberate them into the full dimension of their own creation, which is ultimately God's creation (Eph.1:3–5). So the Good News of Jesus includes also a call to repentance: 'Jesus began his preaching with the message, "Repent for the Kingdom of Heaven is close at hand" ' (Matt.4:17).

Anyone can say, 'Your sins are forgiven,' but only someone with the authority and power of God can say, 'Take up your bed and walk.' These are the words uttered to the paralysed man who was let down through the roof by his friends. So we can see that the good news (evangel) preached by Jesus was not 'hot air' but the fulfilment of the prophecy of Isaiah: 'He has sent me to bring Good News' (Luke 4:18).

The Early Church and the Good News

The Gospel (Good News) encounters a desire to hear the Word and an eagerness to know what must be done in order to be saved. The common qualities we find are those of listening (Acts 2:22), receiving (Acts 8:14–16), and obedience (Acts 6:7).

It is not surprising then, at the beginning of the Acts of the Apostles, that we read, 'I dealt with everything Jesus had done and taught' (Acts 1:1). Notice in this context that the action comes before the teaching, and the implications here are that the Church is meant to continue what Jesus began. This is doing no more than fulfilling the words of Jesus after his resurrection. 'The Good News must first be proclaimed to all the nations' (Mark 13:10).

This is in fact what we find – that the early disciples went about preaching the Good News. 'The people united in welcoming the message Philip preached, either because they had heard of the miracles he worked or because they saw them for themselves' (Acts 8:6). Philip was obviously faithful to the Good News handed down by Jesus, but was also manifesting the signs and wonders that accompanied the message. The Good News preached must have had a definite content, because the Bible uses words like 'preach', 'announce', 'declare', 'speak, 'know', 'teach', 'hear', and 'receive'. The content of the New Testament Good News could be summed up in this way: 'This news is about the Son of God . . . it is about Jesus Christ our Lord . . .' (Rom.1:3).

The most significant passage in the Acts of the Apostles is where Peter explains the Good News to pagans in the house of Cornelius (Acts 10). Peter attests to Cornelius that, 'the good news of peace was brought by Jesus Christ' (Acts 10:36). Peter then proceeds to explain what this Good News is and its implications for the whole household. The basic message that Peter unfolds is an attestation to the person of Jesus. Peter was offering life to Cornelius and his family, not mere empty rhetoric. This is the *kerygma*.

Paul is undoubtedly the main messenger of the Gospel in the early Church of the Scriptures. He was set apart by God to deliver the Good News to the pagans. God saw fit that Paul 'be entrusted with the Good News' (1 Thess. 2:4). Paul's gospel, like that of the Church, centres upon the death and resurrection of Jesus made present by the power of the Holy Spirit. The Good News of the New Testament is the new economy of salvation when it is energetically preached: 'For I am not ashamed of the Good News: it is the power of God saving all who have faith' (Rom.1:16).

In the New Testament the Gospel thrives and bears fruit in the growth of new churches. It is the beginning of a spiritual renewel. Paul emphasizes how the New Testament understanding of the Good News is linked with the Old Testament. He writes in the Epistle to the Romans: '. . . the Good News I preach . . . in which I proclaim Jesus Christ, is the revelation of a mystery kept secret for endless ages . . . This is only what scripture has predicted, and it is all part of the way the eternal God wants things to be' (Rom.16:25-7).

The writings of St John do not contain the words 'good news' (evangel) but, instead, the terms 'word' and 'witness'. In the Apocalypse, however, we find 'good news' mentioned in the context of the final coming of the Kingdom, when God is revealed in glory (Rev.14:6ff).

In short the term 'good news' has rich significance in the New Testament, being used 127 times in all. [11]

Preaching the Good News
It is obvious from the Bible that God worked, powerfully, through the Good News being proclaimed. Yet, firstly, it would be a mistake to judge its validity by apparent or expressed success. We are called to be faithful to the preaching of the Good News, not to its results. In the Acts of the Apostles, for example we find it said that Philip preached 'to a number of Samarian towns' (Acts 8:25). There is no mention of how his preaching was received or even if anyone was converted. So,

in biblical terms, to evangelize does not mean to win converts but simply to proclaim the message irrespective of the results. 'To define evangelism in terms of an effect achieved in the lives of others . . . amounts to saying that the essence of evangelizing is producing converts.' [12]

Secondly, the Bible does not give us methods of how to announce the Good News. It indicates the differing ways that were used by the people of that day, but these are not set for us as a blue-print of how we should tackle evangelism.

Thirdly, evangelism must be true to the basic truths about Jesus and his salvific act. If we move away from these truths, then we simply put across 'hearsays' about God. The evangel must contain the Gospel's account of the life, death and resurrection of Jesus. It must contain the statements made by Jesus. It must contain the statements made by Jesus in his promise of the Holy Spirit and, lastly, it must contain the demands put upon us if we desire to be a disciple of the Good News – the Good News that is the assurance of our final salvation in the future. 'For we must be content to hope that we shall be saved – our salvation . . . is something we must wait for with patience' (Rom 8:24–5).

Everywhere, today, we are faced with bad news. Our papers, our TV and our gossip are filled with it. This troubled world has a need; it needs to hear of the sacrifice made by Jesus over sin. It needs to be aware of the freedom offered in conversion. Some of our Christians have gone out announcing threats; they have preached, not with friendly persuasion, but with verbal coercion. So, our image of God became one of fear – our understanding of the Father became that of an angry old man with a grey beard waiting for us to step out of line so that he could then hit us over the head with a mallet. We often instilled guilt upon an already guilt-ridden people. Many Catholics are weighed down with guilt. Harsh words made the Gospel (evangel) sound like *bad* news. Just as God did not send his Son into the world to condemn it, neither does he send Christians into the world for that purpose. We are supposed to win people, not turn them away. Christians do not condemn, they forgive; they do not assail, they invite. There are millions of people, even among the baptized throngs of the Catholic Church, who have a cancer called sin. The Good News is that the Divine Physician actually has the cure. Yes, it is a cure which has a great price tag attached to it and a great sacrifice. Nevertheless, the Holy Spirit is available to all who come to him.

Surely we must be able to give a first-hand account of the Good News that we bring. That was the way of the biblical disciples. Not all of them had met Jesus in the flesh, but yet they were able to give first-hand information and witness mainly about their own conversion. There is no doubt that today we need a strong and positive sharing of the Good News.

Each generation needs to hear the message of Jesus as though it had never been heard before. Every one of us needs to respond to the message of conversion in repentance. We need to turn to God. This is evangelism. What Jesus and the disciples did in their generation needs to be accomplished again in ours. We need to pray, fast and be optimistic that a new awakening can take place in our lifetime and in our generation. We look for demonstration of the power of the living God in conversion in the lives of ordinary men and women.

4

The Master Builder – 1

Jesus – his plan of action

There is always a tendency to spiritualize Jesus. We have many mental concepts of him, from a timid, meek and mild person, to a judge. While all of these ideas can be true, we rarely think of him as a profound strategist who wished to build a Kingdom. Any evangelization or enrichment of faith to which the Church calls us must always find its pivot in Jesus Christ. The question is constantly posed: how did Jesus set about initiating and building the Kingdom. I realize that our Protestant brothers and sisters have for years put evangelizing and mission at the forefront of activity. I am sure that during the Decade of Evangelization Catholics will hear more and more of the need to evangelize. But do our good theory and ideas get the job done? If we have been successful at evangelizing, then why aren't our churches full? We know that we need to bring the message of the Good News to all people, but are we accomplishing our objective? Pope John Paul II urges us in these words:

> While pointing out and experiencing the present urgency for a re-evangelization, the Church cannot withdraw from the ongoing mission of bringing the Gospel to the multitudes . . . in a specific way this is the missionary work that Jesus entrusted and again entrusts each day to His Church.[1]

Any building, if it is to stand, must be constructed to a plan; otherwise all activity can be aimless or, at best, confused. So, too, with our evangelizing. Serious consideration needs then to be given to new visions and goals. An overall vision of evangelization, and an awareness of realistic goals to be pursued in order to embody that vision, are essential in motivating us towards true evangelization. It is important, then, to attempt an understanding of how Jesus envisaged his task and the strategy he employed to get the job done. Rarely do we look at the strategy of Jesus. It is therefore necessary to go again to the New Testament to clarify for ourselves the practical details of his method. These are the eye-witness accounts of the people who followed him and were taught by him. I realize that the Gospels were written to show us Jesus the Son of God, but we tend to overlook how he taught others so that what he did could be carried into perpetuity.

The first thing we must realize about Jesus is that he was a perfect teacher. He was perfect man and God combined. He came to save the world and to build his Church by the power of the Holy Spirit. 'We have heard him ourselves and we know that he really is the saviour of the world' (John 4:42). His life was geared to winning people for the Father, and he never deviated from that objective. Often in the Church we get sidetracked from our central mission, and this may be the reason for our failure. If the manager of a football team doesn't plan to win, then most certainly his side will be beaten. Jesus was filled with confidence for the future because of his 'winning' mentality; he fulfilled every single training session laid down in the Scriptures. Winning was essential, and so nothing could be left to chance. He had a plan worked out in his mind that was foolproof. Over the next few pages I will analyze this plan and see how it can help us to be more practical in our task of evangelizing today. In doing so I am indebted to the excellent work written by Robert E. Coleman entitled *The Master Plan of Evangelism*.[2]

Jesus' selection process

The great command of Jesus, 'Go teach, make disciples' (Matt. 28:20), was preceded by the words 'Follow me' (Matt. 4:19; Mark 1:18). From the very outset he was going to work through people, starting with the first twelve whom he called to be his followers. So it was not going to be angels who would minister to people; the government of the Father would be placed in the hands of human beings. I am constantly struck by the gigantic aim he proposed for these twelve, namely the conquest of the whole world. 'Go out to the whole world' (Mark 16:16). These were to be the 'light of the world', and the 'salt of the earth' and 'a city built on a hilltop'. He chose rather insignificant men to take a cosmic view of his mission, for upon them he meant to bestow a kingdom. In an essay entitled 'The Twelve Men', which is concerned with the British jury system, G. K. Chesterton wrote:

> Whenever our civilisation wants a library to be catalogued, or a solar system discovered, or any other trifle of this kind, it uses up its specialists. But when it wishes anything done which is really serious, it collects twelve of the ordinary men standing around. The same thing was done, if I remember right, by the Founder of Christianity.

So from the very outset Jesus' concern was not to concentrate on programmes of theory but on people. He would reach the multitudes by using ordinary men. So it is evident from the very beginning that, in order for his message to take root, Jesus intended to call to himself a body of men with whom he could communicate. These men would not be a social body, a club, united for the sake of pleasure or mutual convenience. Nor would they form a political body or be held together by material interests. They would be cemented together at first by his presence and later on by the power of the Holy Spirit. In Catholic theology we use the term 'mystical body' of this group of people. If it was to have continuity, it needed leadership and members. If it was a vineyard, as Jesus described it, it needed labourers; if it was a net, it needed fishermen; if it was a field, it needed workers; if it was a herd or flock, it needed shepherds and sheep. So, however remarkable it may seem, before he even preached a sermon he called men to be at his side. *People* were going to be his method and strategy.

The interesting fact about this choice of Jesus is that there is no element of haste in his decision. 'As he was walking by the Sea of Galilee he saw two brothers, . . . Peter and Andrew . . . ; they were making a cast in the lake with their net' (Matt. 4:18). This passage suggests that Jesus observed these men at work. He would have assessed them in their ordinary jobs and recognized their efficiency. He was determined to get the right men for the job and that demanded great observance and astuteness on his part. He did not have access to files or *curricula vitae* but, like us, he did have personal encounters with people. It seems, from the Scriptures, that he interviewed for the jobs available by observing his men at their ordinary tasks. So the right person for the job in hand was chosen, not because of his academic or theological background, but to fulfil the ultimate purpose of spreading the Kingdom. One quality that all of them possessed was an adventurous spirit and a willingness to follow Jesus into the insecurity of an evolving vision. Luke shares with us, that at the heart of Jesus' decision was prayer: 'Now it was about this time that he went out into the hills to pray; and he spent the whole night in prayer to God. When day came he summoned his disciples and picked out twelve of them' (Luke 6:12–13).

These men were a cross-section of society,[3] varying in character from Peter who was impulsive, courageous, impetuous and boastful, to Judas the avaricious one. None of the men selected by Jesus held prominent positions in the synagogue; more significantly, none of them were priests. They were not wealthy, nor did they come from noble families. They were just ordinary people. All of them came from the northern part of the country except Judas, who hailed from the southern region of Judea.

This north/south divide would cause problems for Jesus later on – maybe in a similar way to the north/south divide in present-day Britain.[4] The men he chose were not well educated; they weren't even very bright, if we judge from their reaction to supernatural things. Finding even the most elementary examples and comparisons beyond their reach, they would turn to Jesus and ask: 'Explain the parable to us' (Matt. 13:36). Yet Jesus saw in these men the potential for leadership, and assigned to them special roles. Jesus called them to follow him, to leave behind their ordinary lives, and to be as mobile as he was. The one quality that Jesus asked of them was that they be teachable. Like the clay that is pliable in the hand of the potter, they too were going to be moulded by Jesus into preachers of the Kingdom.

So the first strategic move made by Jesus contained an elementary, fundamental principle – namely, concentration upon a few.[5] In one of the greatest books written this century, Schumacher advocates that the smaller the group, the more productive the product;[6] this principle is effective. So, however symbolic the number twelve is, Jesus intended to concentrate his efforts upon this select group. This does not mean that he excluded or neglected other people. Jesus did not spare himself in his ministry to the masses. He continuously preached the Gospel, healed the sick and cast out demons – so much so that often he didn't even have time to eat (Mark 6:31). He did not shirk his responsibility in evangelistic fervour, and was so successful in his public ministry that large crowds followed him. The priests of the day were jealous because of his personal ability to attract the crowds and his popularity among the masses. He could easily have encouraged a public uprising and become a political figure, but he had not come to play to the popular vote.

After being with the crowds, Jesus would always return to the twelve and encourage them not to be deceived by popular acclaim. One has only to read history to grasp an insight into how temperamental crowds are; how easily they can be swayed.

Jesus ministered to the crowds, but he wished to train the twelve. The crowds would defeat his strategy, but the twelve would, eventually, understand his purpose. It was on these few that the evangelization of the world depended. It is interesting to note that, although he was the greatest evangelist that ever lived, Jesus was surprisingly unsuccessful in converting people. Comparatively few really grasped the meaning of the Gospel, which seems to indicate that he concentrated much of his efforts on the twelve. But, since he came to save the world, why didn't he capitalize on the many opportunities that came his way? The answer to this question is surely not contained in mass evangelism but in the sowing of seeds among the few so that they in turn could lead. He wanted the Kingdom to be built on strong solid foundations – the small band of twelve. This was his realistic strategy.

Today

In our modern day we live in a consumers' society where everything is fast. We can obtain fast food, drive fast cars and are bombarded by fast commercials. This, inevitably, colours our attitudes. We may seek fast evangelism. But there are no short cuts that can be taken in our concern to evangelize. We see no haste in the strategy of Jesus. Jesus does not start in the middle or at the end, he makes no presumptions as to where the twelve are, but sets out from scratch.[7] It is necessary for us also to start from scratch, leaving nothing to chance. The results of fast evangelism are people coming in the front door and disappearing through the back one, slipping through without really understanding. In Catholic churches, today, we have hundreds of people attending. In fact, statistically speaking, in Britain and Ireland we have the largest attendance of any single denomination. When attempting to evangelize the crowds, we may have some successes, but few roots go deep. If the strategy of Jesus is to teach us anything, surely it must be the selection of a few teachable people so that they can become the leaven in the dough. This will entail raising up trained leadership, not just a 'holy huddle' or 'friends of Father' but people who are dedicated to get the job done. Yes, it is possible that the priest or parish leader may be accused of favouritism, but it has to be said that Jesus concentrated his life on a few so that trained leadership could emerge. The few selected for training must not be people who will use it for their own edification or self-satisfaction but those who will use it to proclaim the Gospel to others. Christianity can multiply much more easily and effectively if good leadership is present.

I find in my own life as an evangelist that to mention the words 'programme' or 'package' is enough to make most priests, bishops and people switch off. Everything today is supplied in a handy package that often doesn't work or, at best, works for a time. We can get so bogged down with programmes. The need, therefore, is to set aside people for the ministry of evangelist. We have understood, very well, the need for pastors, counsellors and catechists, to mention but a few, but – in the Catholic Church – we haven't woken up to the need for evangelists in their own right. Our first priority then surely is to convince bishops and priests of the need to get good reliable leaders in this area of evangelization. These people will not necessarily come from the ranks of the intellectuals or higher classes, but from ordinary people who are willing to follow Christ. Here is where we begin to follow Jesus. At first it will be slow, even tedious, and with few results, but the fruits will begin to emerge. We, as leaders and priests in the Church, must decide whether we want immediate popular acclaim or continuing proclamation of the Gospel after we are gone. The time is now ripe.

Jesus' training programme

Having selected his chosen band of people Jesus set about the task of training them. Here, too, he had a method and a strategy; they were going to be trained on the job. When I look at the strategy of Jesus I am constantly astounded at its natural simplicity. Jesus would have been looked upon in his day as another rabbi (teacher) to whom students would attach themselves. But Jesus' students would be life-long learners, unlike those who would graduate from other rabbis after a few years. His students were called, not to a set of good philosophies or ideas, but to follow him as a person. Jesus had no university or seminary to which he could enrol his apostles. He was his own school and he drew his apostles close to himself. His classes were not communicated in terms of lectures but in his own living personality as he stayed with them. They belonged to him and he to them. They walked with him, talked with him and observed him at work. In this way the mysteries of the Kingdom were unfolded. When they saw the Kingdom being proclaimed by signs and wonders, then their demand for explanations was much more directed towards seeking understanding. We can see from the Bible that this was really so for John and Andrew, when they were invited to 'come and see' (John 1:39). When people are enquiring about our community I inevitably say, 'Why don't you come and work with us for a period?' It is when they see things at first-hand that discernment is achieved. One living experience is better than all the words ever written. When Jesus' apostles worked with him, they then could enrol in his school. By his side they had access to him and could ask anything they needed to know.

Later he would ask them to 'go forth', but he didn't immediately show them the task in the hope that they would get on with it. Before they could go out, or were equipped to do so, they had to have constant contact with Jesus. From the outset of his ministry they were with him, but during the second and third years, as he came closer to facing the cross, he spent increasingly long periods with them. He took them away from the public into the hills to pray and created plenty of opportunities to be close to them. Even before his entry into Jerusalem he took them aside to rest and pray, so it is no surprise to find that during Holy Week he never let them out of his sight.

Isn't this all very natural? I remember well that when my

own father was dying, all the family kept a bedside vigil to be with him. During those last hours of his life my father spoke to us all and we have all treasured those dying words. They were words of encouragement, exhortation and warning and, despite my youth and lack of appreciation of death at that time, I remember well what he said to me. Moments like these are precious, and words uttered at time of death find a more ready home in us. Likewise, with Jesus, it was only at this tragic time that realization came to the apostles. Maybe this is the reason why so much is written about the last days and months of Jesus' life. The apostles had an acute awareness of each treasured moment.

After the resurrection all Jesus' appearances were to his followers, in particular the twelve. Not a single unbeliever saw the Risen Jesus. The twelve needed to be reassured in their faith and in their mission to evangelize. Jesus had given so much time to the apostles – he literally 'wasted' time with them. Other people were clamouring for his time and attention but, without pushing these aside or neglecting them, he dedicated most of his precious time to the training of the twelve.

Jesus and commitment

Probably one of the most effective training tools that Jesus used was his insistence upon commitment and faithfulness to it. He realized that these men who followed him did not possess every quality of mind and body, but one thing he asked for, which all of them did possess, was their ability to be loyal. One example of this loyalty is Matthew. He was a publican under the government of Herod and an employee of Rome. A publican was one who sold out his own people and collected taxes for a foreign power, retaining for himself probably a fairly large percentage. He would have been held in contempt by his own nation yet at the same time he had the power and legal authority of the Roman government behind him. We meet Matthew near Capernaum where he is collecting taxes. His submission to Jesus was immediate. The Gospel relates: 'As Jesus was walking on from there he saw a man named Matthew sitting by the customs house, and he said to him "Follow Me". And he got up and followed him' (Matt. 9:9).

Matthew, who must have been relatively wealthy, would now have little to look forward to but poverty and persecution. His response was all the more remarkable, because he had been dealing in high finance, which can tend to attract unscrupulous and unethical people. This man, who had suffocated all patriotism in himself, ended up by becoming the most patriotic of his people through his obedience. We can see from this one incident that Jesus 'meant business'. He didn't start by asking his disciples to make professions of faith, but he did ask for total commitment. So from the earliest moment it was made clear by Jesus that becoming a disciple involved a surrender of one's whole life to his sovereignity. It was not a case of having one foot in the camp and another elsewhere – there was a price-tag attached. This was strong teaching, and not many of those who came to hear him were able to follow. It was to their own advantage to have their stomachs filled, their sickness healed and their oppressions lifted, but when they were asked for total commitment most of them left.

It is interesting to note that Jesus didn't go running after disciples just to keep his numbers up. As in the case of the rich young man, whose face fell when confronted with the Gospel, Jesus 'looked steadily at him and loved him' as he walked away (Mark 10:17–22). Jesus' call to commitment was, 'If anyone wants to be a follower of mine, let him renounce himself and take up his cross' (Mark 8:34).

When all those who had sought popular acclaim had left Jesus, there remained only the twelve; they continued faithful and loyal. Even so, they did not understand clearly where it was all leading. It was still hard for them to accept their lowly position. Some of them wanted prominent positions, others were indignant. They were still in a learning position, and Jesus patiently endured their human shortcomings. Gradually they were realizing his purpose and becoming equipped for leadership, through their willingness to put up with hardship. Commitment and loyalty leads to maturity; selflessness puts childishness to flight. Loyalty was the means by which greater truth was revealed. Jesus was truth personified, and this instilled confidence and trust. It was loyalty to his Father's will that propelled Jesus on. He didn't ask the twelve to do anything which he, in turn, was not prepared to do. He came on earth for a purpose – 'to give his life as a ransom for many' (Mark 10:45) – and to this he dedicated his time and efforts, even to the cross.

Today

Recently, while working in a parish, I heard the door-bell ring. On opening the door I saw a man of the road standing there. He was asking for some money. I put my hand in my pocket and took out a pound coin. He accepted it gratefully and left. As I stood there with my thoughts, I came to realize that it is so easy sometimes to escape responsibility by giving money. It avoids the consuming effort of giving our time. Time is the most expensive commodity in our Western society. We now have more technology and automation than ever before, yet we seem to have less and less time.

Take a trip down any High Street and we will quickly see the rush that we are all caught in. But in any building programme time is essential. Jesus quickly realized the value in training of spending time with the selected few. In the Church we lack understanding of this principle; it is easier to push papers through photocopiers in the false hope that imparting information will be sufficient. The building of strong men and women is not easy. It requires personal proximity much in the same way as healthy children come from homes where both mother and father show them close attention. We cannot grow by proxy. The implications for us, practically, in our Catholic tradition are many. It demands that bishops and priests should spend much more time together for mutual encouragement and support. I realize that there are many pressing issues and demands, but these leaders will not in turn be able to lead unless inspiration is gleaned from mutual support. Among our clergy 'burn out' is the biggest problem, in my estimation, and this results from lack of personal association.

I believe we have failed, tragically, in our attempts to nurture our people. Many priests have tried to do it alone, but it is impossible to minister effectively to five or six hundred people. We can preach the Gospel to them but in no way can we, adequately, be personally involved with such large numbers. I sometimes say, maybe rather cynically, 'When a person is searching for God the Catholic Church is great, but when that person has found God we don't know what to do with them.' By this I mean that when we evangelize we have a responsibility to those who are evangelized. We cannot just leave them in the hope that coming to Mass will be sufficient. We need a proper nurturing system and this, inevitably, calls for a trained leadership. To create this leadership will mean spending lots of time with a selected few. If Jesus, the Son of God, found it necessary to employ this principle, will anything less be expected of us? We cannot afford to have a 'production line' mentality, or a hit-and-miss strategy; this only exhausts us.

Lastly, we made our people what they are today. In the past we only asked them to turn out for Mass. Now we are asking for their involvement. People are not like machines that can change quickly if programmed correctly. It is going to take time and clear direction before they can appreciate the way we wish them to go. This has to be a gradual and patient process.

Our commitment
Virtually everything in our society works against commitment. There is a great fear among people; we don't want to get trapped. Commitment is our fundamental decision in regard to God. Spiritually speaking it marks the ending of the old and the emergence of the new. This decision to allow ourselves to be remade is neither a static nor a once-and-finished event. It is both a moment and a process. When we make a commitment

to follow the Lord, our lives are no longer organized around our own needs or the dictates of others. They belong to the Lord. Our commitment then is the first step of entry into the Kingdom. Evangelism is to this end. The most controversial question at stake in the world, and even in the Church, is whether men and women will commit themselves to Jesus and live under the banner of the Kingdom. In our preaching we must ask this question and aim it right at the heart of individuals and communities. Evangelism confronts each person with the decisive choice about Jesus. But commitment cannot be an end in itself. It marks the birth of an active, practical life in the Church and in the world. The connection between commitment to Jesus and active responsibility cannot be emphasized enough. It puts to rest the notion that turning up to Mass is enough to fulfil our obligations to God. Few of our people see involvement as necessary; most leave it to the 'faithful few'.

As commitment grows, then so does our practical involvement.[8] It is very difficult to build a solid foundation in any parish or community when commitment is either not present or is haphazard and intermittent. Commitment is our covenant with God and the faith community. When people move away from commitment any building programme, however good, is thrown off balance, and the result is frustration and apathy.

There are certain facts that are worth noting when we look at the Church today with a view to evangelizing. On the positive side, there is a tremendous potential for evangelizing, not seen before. There are many people in our churches who have the potential but are uncommitted to Jesus. In those who are committed there is tremendous interest, eagerness and enthusiasm. We need to create structures so that the energy of these people can be harnessed. We cannot afford to have them build with one hand tied behind their backs. Also, I believe, we must challenge those who are lukewarm even at the expense of losing them. The Scriptures make this challenge: 'I know all about you: how you are neither hot nor cold. I wish you were one or the other, but since you are neither, but only lukewarm, I will spit you out of my mouth' (Rev. 3:15–16). In different places throughout the Western world one can hear the cry of priests and people, 'No matter what we put on people don't attend as they should.' I'm sure there are many reasons for this happening, but one answer could be that individuals are unevangelized and hence do not see a necessity to grow or be committed to each other.

The call to commitment today therefore cannot be a matter of indifference.[9] Priests and people have sometimes settled for a happy medium in our faith, even a contented complacency, but this only leads to mediocrity. We must not look upon this situation negatively or in despair, but instead call for action in commitment.[10] And not only our lay people; questions must also be seriously aimed at bishops, priests and religious. No one, not even the Pope, is above the call to commitment, and it would be a tragedy to exclude any group.

'It is when the firm principle of commitment is accepted that we can endeavour to build the Kingdom "this side of eternity".'[11]

5

The Master Builder – 2

Jesus as example

If one is to spend much time with someone then, obviously,
sooner or later we shall show our true colours by what we do.
If this is true in the natural order, then it must also be true in
the spiritual realm. Part of the apostles' training as evangelizers
must have been their spiritual development. In many instances
we verbalize the need, but Jesus' offered himself as an example
which showed the apostles their need. We all spend a great
deal of our time talking with other people but, strangely, often
little that is said stays in our memory. Studies have shown that
even good friends find it difficult to communicate at a deep
level, and some married people discover that their level of
communication is inadequate.[1]

Jesus and prayer

Jesus did not force lessons upon people but rather taught by
example and waited patiently for the convenient opening in
which to explain his actions. The gospels explicitly tell us that
Jesus was a man of prayer. He withdrew into solitude to pray
(Mark 6:46), and before he sets out to preach the Gospel we
see him at prayer (Mark 1:35). The Scriptures almost always
give in some detail the external circumstances of Jesus at
prayer. We are not told that Jesus ever went to the temple to
pray, though this does not rule out the possibility that he did
pray there. Maybe this indicates that Jesus freed prayer from

its old forms. Prayer filled his life. Busy all day long with spreading the Good News he still found time to pray. We should not be surprised then to discover that during moments of crisis and at important times, prayer and Jesus are closely connected.

Jesus prayed before the choosing of the twelve (Luke 6:12). He prayed before he began preaching in Galilee. He prayed before Peter's confession of faith. He prayed especially for Peter (Luke 22:31). During his ministry he laid his hands on others while praying (Mark 9:29). He who drove out so many unclean spirits said that this could not be done except by fasting and prayer (Mark 9:29). At times the development of his ministry or the accomplishment of his works drew forth from him prayers of thanksgiving to the Father (Matt. 11:25; Luke 10:21; John 11:41).

Notice that not once did he make his disciples pray. He just kept praying until at last they could contain their hunger no longer and asked him to teach them how to pray. The question came from the twelve, indicating that they were now ready to listen and to hear. Jesus must have jumped at this opportunity of holding before them his model of prayer. It is interesting to note that he gave them a formula, neat and tidy. It was almost as if he was getting them into practice so that later on their own prayer life could develop. It is also interesting to note that in this first prayer taught by Jesus there is no sentimentality, piousness or rhetoric. It is simple, direct and filled with nobility and sureness. It contains simple praise and intercession.

Jesus and Scripture

As well as unfolding his total dependence upon his Father in prayer, Jesus constantly showed his knowledge of the Scriptures. As a Jew he was steeped in the Old Testament. In preaching and teaching the Scriptures he made a distinction between the disciples, who had already committed themselves to him and who 'believed', at least in principle, and the masses who turned up to hear him. Jesus put himself out to explain to the twelve the meaning of particular texts. He was showing them the absolute necessity of being able to understand and use the Scriptures to demonstrate their preaching, because the Word of God truly does confront people with God. The disciples could see how Jesus used the Old Testament to initiate and support his pronouncements. They would have clearly seen that the words written in the Old Testament and his words complemented each other and, later on, would follow these two principles in their own ministry. He was showing them that true evangelization must be scripturally based. It must never be our own words, for it is God's Gospel.

Through all of this Jesus was giving them the ultimate example in how to spread the Gospel. He was a living witness to God-centred incidents of evangelism. He did not use massive publicity, gimmicks or hard-sell techniques; everything about him was authentic and realistic. The disciples learned quickly that, out of deep scriptural prayer, God the Father opened channels through which the message could be preached. By Jesus' example they learned the best methods of approaching people. He understood individual needs and responded compassionately. He won people's confidence and trust and called them to a decision. Without any 'DIY' manual, his method was real and practical.

Jesus and the Spirit

Yet, despite all these worthwhile elements of training and skills, Jesus knew these weren't enough. Unless he loved them, all would be lost. Later they would receive the Holy Spirit of love at Pentecost, but now it was important that he gave himself to them in unselfish love.

He could not teach them that 'God so loved the world' (John 3:16) unless he somehow embodied that love. All teaching and example is useless unless it is underpinned by love. He showed them by example that love which existed between himself and the Father and how it propelled him to love others. He demonstrated this love to the twelve in many ways, but none more powerful than when he washed their feet. Having given this example he could say with clarity and conviction, 'As you sent me into the world, I have sent them into the world, and for their sake I consecrate myself so that they too may be consecrated in truth' (John 17:18–19).

Jesus' demonstrations of love showed them that his Gospel was true – he lived what he believed. Love is always the credential of true evangelism. How else can free people be led to make a free choice? But no person can have this love unless by the power of the Holy Spirit. Jesus' life was embued by the Holy Spirit, 'Jesus was under the immediate tutelage of the Spirit.'[2] He was not going to leave them orphans; he promised them that they too would receive the Holy Spirit. This Spirit would enlighten them in all ways and help them to appreciate all that he was now doing and teaching. He showed clearly that evangelism was and is the Holy Spirit's work. The apostles had gleaned their courage and strength from Jesus, but the reality was that he was not going to be around much longer. Therefore he had to explain to them the Holy Spirit, the compensation for their loss. In the power of the Spirit he would not forsake them (Matt. 28:20; John 14:16). Evangelism was a burning compulsion within Jesus, and when Pentecost day came, the twelve also would be given 'fire in their bellies'.

Today

In any outreach today these three principles, the Holy Spirit, Scripture and prayer, must be present. Unless these are active, our strategies and ideas will be inoculated with the kiss of death. There are, of course, some active churches based on charismatic leadership, which although very productive in the short term can, in the long term, be unproductive. As we look at the history of different revivals, we can see how quickly some of them petered out. Some lasted only as long as the dynamic leader. Modern methods of communications, imaginative visions, well known speakers and meticulously planned programmes are no substitute for the vital elements of prayer, Scripture and the Holy Spirit. Let's look at these a little closer.

Prayer and us

The Catholic Church will not be able to respond adequately to crisis unless those with responsibilities are people of prayer – bishops, priests, religious and lay leaders. I realize that we are blessed with many men and women of great faith, and to some extent the Church is relatively healthy. Yet one cannot deny that trends inside and out are battering her. Great numbers of Catholics are unevangelized and haphazardly incorporated into local communities. These then become vulnerable, being tossed about by every new doctrine. This could be said of every era in the life of the Church. However, prayer, my first principle, brings about great cohesion, unity and commitment and helps people grow strong. In any evangelizing situation we will be confronted very quickly by the powers of evil: 'Despite every difficulty, delay and contradiction caused by the limits of human nature, by sin and by the evil one, the Church knows,'[3] that by prayer and fasting these can be counteracted.

In essence, this means that those of us who are leaders will only have people prepared to follow us when they see us as men and women of prayer and fasting. When we become an example of a lived spirituality, we shall win the healthy admiration and trust of those in our care, thus opening the door for imparting the message. This was Jesus' method.

Apart from the good example given by a praying person, I believe it is imperative to break the stronghold of Satan by the power of conscious, deliberate intercession. 'Our battle is not against human forces but against the principalities and powers' (Eph. 6:12). I do not want to labour this point, already dealt with earlier in this book, but it is well to remember that Satan inspired humankind's original turning from God, and he continues to alienate us from God. Let us not forget that evangelism is about the breaking in of the Kingdom of God into ordinary lives.

I am reminded, constantly, that virtually all renewal movements in the Catholic tradition were preceded by intense prayer and intercession. All evangelists grow out of a deep spiritual resource centre. I am reminded of St Alphonsus, the founder of the Redemptorists, to quote but one; hand in hand with all their missionary activity, even to this day, is an intercessory order of nuns. If these great men and women saw this element of intercession as imperative, surely the same is to be expected of us today as we embark upon a new wave of evangelism.[4] I am firmly convinced that, for us Catholics, there is no substitute for intercession and prayer made before the Blessed Sacrament.

On a visit recently to Father Michael Eivers' parish in Pembroke Pines, Florida, I found that his parish chapel is open eighteen hours each day for intercession. Michael attributes all their evangelizing successes to the power of this type of prayer.[5] Pastor Cho, in Korea, has 10,000 people gathering twice weekly for intercession. Prayer and intercession bridge the ecumenical divide.[6] Going hand in hand, therefore, with any attempt at outreach is the necessity for intercession.

Often in our parishes we have sick or retired people who sometimes feel isolated. They have become less mobile so it is more difficult for them to evangelize actively. Could we not form some of these people into a spiritual army of intercession? 'Our prayer does not depend on our physical energy but on our love for God and our surrender to Him.'[7] This would not mean that we could then opt out, but simply that older people and sick people are often responsive to God's grace and more able to evaluate things accurately. This equips them to pray for the work of evangelism more effectively.

The Bible and us

What about Scripture, my second principle? The life of Jesus was steeped in Scripture, and if we are to evangelize this must also be true of us. Nothing is more important to the Christian faith than that which has to do with the basis of our religious knowledge. For any Christian the root question is: from where do I get my knowledge on which to base my faith? When all has been said and done, the only true and dependable source for Christianity lies in the book that we call the Bible. I realize that after the Reformation Catholics were discouraged from reading the Bible, but the Church has always venerated the Scriptures and recognized them as indispensable elements in theology, preaching the Word and catechetical instruction. What had gone wrong since the Middle Ages was not the Bible's role in the official Church but its role in the life of individuals.

Evangelization then means, essentially, an attempt to liberate the Bible from its splendid isolation. Our lack of contact with God's inspired word leads to great impoverishment. I do not wish to confuse biblical revival in evangelism with biblical research. The rise in modern science has greatly enhanced biblical studies, but all of this new knowledge can neither cause nor bring about a biblical revival. The purpose of Scripture in evangelism is to be the food by which our lives are nourished day by day. In the Scriptures God speaks to us in a language that we can understand. 'Ignorance of the Scriptures is ignorance of Christ,' says the Vatican Council.[8] 'St Chrysostom says, "When we receive a letter from a friend we pay close attention not only to the content of it but also to the affection of the writer expressed in it." '[9]

The practical implications of all of this is that close attention must be paid to the word of God in evangelizing. We need more parish and group-structured teaching and certainly a better applied readers' programme for those who are responsible for proclaiming the word at public liturgies. We also need training facilities available to help those in the front line of evangelism to become better equipped to share the Good News which is rooted in the Scriptures. Evangelism and the Scriptures go hand in hand.

The Spirit and us

On this, my third principle, I have written at length in chapter 2. However, at the risk of repeating myself, I think it is necessary to say something here.

> The only power God recognizes in His Church is the power of the Spirit; whereas the only power actually recognized today by the majority . . . is the power of man. God does His work by the operation of the Spirit, while Christian leaders attempt to do theirs by the power of the trained and devoted mind . . .
>
> Everything that men do in their own strength and by means of their own abilities is done for time alone . . . it is a solemn thought that some of us who fancy ourselves to be important evangelical leaders may find at last we have been but busy harvesters of stubble.[10]

Any evangelism which does not have the Holy Spirit as its power is folly. We cannot possibly give away what we haven't got. The guiding aspect of the Spirit is uniquely important. One of the great tragedies of our time is that we have too many so-called 'discerning' men and women in the Church of liberal and conservative persuasions and not enough people who are led by the Spirit. This failure to submit in surrender to the Holy Spirit is the cause of emptiness and lack of fruit in much of our evangelizing today. We have so many realists and not enough prepared to take risks for God. We need to remain wide open to all that God wants of us.

The question is always asked, 'How will I know if I have the Holy Spirit?' I realize that his question must not be given a glib answer, but part of the response must be that if the Spirit of God is within us he will wish to make Jesus known and loved – we shall be aglow with the Spirit. The Holy Spirit is given to us, not just for great spiritual experiences, nor lengthy discussions on the finer points of theology, but that we might be witnesses to Jesus. We witness in many ways, but all must be stabilized and formed by love. I will illustrate my point with a little story.

A couple, who are good friends of mine, married some ten years ago. They longed to have a child but couldn't. Eventually the woman conceived and gave birth to a baby boy. He was perfectly formed – his little toes, feet, hands, eyes and ears, everything – but he was dead. It was a time of great sadness. We in evangelism can be like that sometimes. We can have all the right things but lack the life of the Spirit: 'If I have all . . . but am without love it will do me no good whatever' (1 Cor. 13:1–3). Evangelism must contain the love of God – the Spirit – so that we can demonstrate our sincerity.

As we can appreciate, example is not enough. There has to come a time for action. To disregard acquired knowledge and not afford it the scope and outlet it needs, is nothing short of nullifying it. The knowledge and the example given by Jesus to the twelve had to be applied by them in concrete situations. After all Jesus was training them to do the job, so it was important that everything could be applied practically.

Jesus and job allocation

Jesus was building for the time when his apostles would take over. I am assuming that one of the reasons why he was constantly telling them about his forthcoming death was to jolt them into an appreciation that soon they would be on their own. He was patiently implanting seeds. Let us not forget that when he called them he did not give them everything at once; he didn't tell them, 'I want you to know that you have got a three-year apprenticeship.' When they had an experience of God, then he would drop the 'bombshell'. On the other hand, he didn't dissuade them from taking impulsive action. For example, Andrew brought Peter, and Philip brought Nathaniel. Jesus used his apostles to build up the work. They were allocated the jobs of getting food, arranging accommodation. He even allowed them to baptize: 'Though it was his disciples who baptized not Jesus himself' (John 4:2). Apart from these occasions, the gospels do not tell us that the disciples did much more than this. They seemed initially to watch and observe while he was putting before them the vision that one day he would expect them to be fishers of men (Mark 1:17; Matt. 4:19; Luke 5:10). In fact, even after he formally appointed the twelve (Mark 3:14) there is no evidence that they operated on their own.

However, in Mark (6:7–13) we read, 'He summoned the twelve and began to send them out in pairs giving them authority over the unclean spirits . . . So they set off to preach repentance, and they cast out many devils and anointed many sick people with oil and cured them.' Here it is set out how they were to proclaim the victory of the Kingdom. They were called to share the healing power, authority and the triumph of Jesus. Now was the time to become 'fishers of men'. They were to be fishers, not by trapping or cajoling, and even less by tyrannizing people; they were simply called to proclaim the Kingdom with power. They had rested in the security of Jesus' ministry for long enough, and now they had to find their own wings. Nevertheless he did brief them: they were to preach – heal – deliver – proclaim the Kingdom. He also instructed them to go two by two for companionship and safety. They were to stay in the same house in any place they visited – to avoid jealousy – and to appreciate the hospitality offered them by not being fussy about what they ate. No pressure was to be put on people. Finally, they were to be totally dependent on God to supply their needs.

On this first sortie they were not to go to 'pagan territory' (Matt. 10:5). In other words they were to go to their own people (Jews), who would be more likely to give them a good reception. This was sound advice. It recalls to my mind my first parish priest telling me to go to people who would receive me well and that would give me encouragement. In effect, Jesus was asking them to concentrate on the 'open' ones.

The briefing Jesus gave was not 'pie in the sky'. He didn't promise that everyone would hear or even be receptive, but he did promise them that God would be faithful and would not desert them. They were to be as 'cunning as serpents and yet as harmless as doves' (Matt. 10:16). They were going to proclaim a revolutionary gospel, so it involved no easy option for the twelve. They were already aware that Jesus and his message had been rejected, and they could not expect anything different. They knew that he was not abdicating his responsibility but rather delegating. These twelve disciples returned, and a few months later seventy-two of Jesus' followers were sent out. Their briefings were of a similar nature, with one exception – they were to go into every town where he himself would visit (Luke 10:1).

After Jesus' resurrection the main commission he gave to his disciples was to go out. However, he got them started while he was with them. This was a wise move, because he could evaluate their progress. Their field assignment completed it was now time to sit around the table and review their progress. They came back rejoicing, ' "Lord," they said, "even the devils submit to us when we use your name" ' (Luke 10:17). Nothing, I'm sure, could have given Jesus greater joy, yet he had a word of warning, 'Rejoice rather that your names are written in Heaven' (Luke 10:20).

What a wise person Jesus was. How fame and public acclaim can go quickly to people's heads – even the disciples'! Jesus brought them back to reality. This was on-the-job training. Jesus allowed them to work and make observances of their own, and then used these as a starting point for discipleship and wisdom. (One always appreciates a lesson more after one has had the opportunity to apply it.) His plan of teaching by assignment and constant evaluation will bring out the best in his disciples.

Jesus' intention through all of this was that his disciples would multiply. Through them others would come to know his name. He was, if you like, exemplifying the mustard seed which he had explained to them early in his ministry (Matt. 13:18–23). Starting in a small way, his gospel of the Kingdom would be proclaimed world-wide, and his Church would be built. He had the confidence in this little band to say, 'You are Peter and upon this rock I will build by Church' (Matt. 16:18).

Just as any army has to have a 'beach-head' when fighting a war, these twelve would be his. He depended upon their faithfulness for the task to be fulfilled. Through the Holy Spirit and the command, 'Go out and bear fruit' (John 15:16), his Church would win. This was his plan, his only plan. Again, in all of this, leadership is vital. Jesus knew that the harvest was ripe, but without good leadership the crops could not be saved. That is why he asks us to pray for 'labourers' (Matt. 9:37). In the Catholic tradition this has meant praying for more priests. But while this is still relevant, good lay leadership is also needed. We are building for the future, and the test of any evangelizing is not just the present moment but how effective the work will be as it continues into the next generation. Similarly, our ambition should not be just getting more into the pews, or paying off debts but, rather, training more people who, in turn, will bring others to Christ. We are grateful to the early disciples to whom, beginning with that first sortie out into the world, multitudes have been added.

Today

It is not good enough to stay with the theory of evangelism and remain at the level of the ideal. We are too aware of the many committees set up to analyze problem areas in the Church and, while these are necessary and can be productive, it is important for the work to get off the ground. Having provided initial training we need to send people out. There is a fear in some quarters of the Catholic Church regarding lay people evangelizing, a fear that it will get out of control. Priests have tried to control it in the past but, paradoxically, we lose the very thing we try to order. People do need to start somewhere, and our fear of taking risks and failure must not hinder the work of evangelism. The theory must be given tangible expression by those who are following Jesus. The best way to do this is to give practical work assignments and expect these to be carried out. In following the pattern laid down by Jesus to the twelve, I see five classes of people: (a) receptive, (b) interested, (c) indifferent, (d) resistant and (e) hostile. May I now suggest a practical strategy for any trained group to get started. They could visit (a) receptive people once a month, (b) interested people every two months, (c) indifferent people every six months, (d) resistant people every nine months, and (e) hostile people once a year. As people will change in their receptivity, so they can be reclassified and visited accordingly.[11] If the Jehovah Witnesses and Mormons can do this then surely so can we.

However, the fact that people begin is no indication that they will continue. Once nerves are overcome we need to keep them moving. We cannot ask people to become involved practically and then lose contact with them. Leaders, especially priests, must be in the melting-pot as well. A quick blessing and allowing them to go forth will not suffice. Training is always needed and, especially, the personal contact and encouragement. 'Pastors must always acknowledge that their ministry is fundamentally ordered to the service of the entire people of God.'[12] No true evangelizing will take place if pastors and leaders abdicate the central calling of the Church. Giving it over to someone else because of lack of interest is not real delegation and will, ultimately, 'make a rod for our own back'. We must not assume that the work will get done merely because a willing worker has been shown how to do it. There is always great frustration in the ministry of evangelism, and this calls for a realistic and competent understanding of people if we are to guard against discouragement and defeat. On the other hand, great experiences will present themselves, so assessment is always valuable. In industry they call it the 'big E', for evaluation. This evaluation keeps the vision clear in people's minds. It will show us, through experience, what is working and what needs to be changed. Evaluation will pin-point abilities and weakness in any evangelizing group.

Supervision is also very important as part of any evaluation process. People can get on 'ego trips'. Or we can fail because of making excuses for ourselves, failing to take on board new things, justifying ourselves by what we do already. We must not rest satisfied with the first fruits. Going out in evangelism brings maturity and confidence to the evangelizer. We cannot afford to settle for second best.

The early Church did not settle for small victories. Their vision was to spread the message into all strata of the known world. Their impact was such that they, eventually, found their way into the Roman Emperor's palace. We need to be open, ready, and even searching, if we are to multiply. To do any other is simply to remain dormant. When can we realize that evangelism is not done by a programme but through personal contact? God always has to be personal. People are God's method.[13] People do not grow in large groups, therefore we have to create small groups with the idea of multiplication. In the small groups greater selection, greater training, greater example and job allocation can become reality. Multiplication will then follow.

Finally, we can see from the life and teaching of Jesus that he was consciously aware of the many pitfalls. He sent out disciples who were 'tuned in' to the problems of the day. To avoid significant failure Jesus put before them clear warnings of what they were going to encounter. He read, carefully, the 'signs of the times'. If we are adopting a realistic approach to evangelism then we too need to be aware of the world we are stepping into. There will be dangers to be faced. These dangers I call stumbling blocks.

6

The Stumbling Blocks

A priest friend said to me recently, 'The problem with our people today is that they have a "crisis of faith".' He didn't mean that, today, we have less faith than in previous generations, but that our faith is being bombarded each day from all quarters. Therefore, in this chapter, I intend to look at some of the main hindrances to effective evangelizing taking place. We, as Christians, are involved in the world each day, and to be truly Christian means to be beyond all things, yet at the same time in the midst of them. There are stumbling blocks in the world and in the Church today which can suck us in and make us less disposed to God. I realize that this whole topic would need a book dedicated to it. However, it is necessary here to look at some of the main areas of concern.

Secularism

We are all born into a particular society and culture. This involves thoughts, feelings and actions. Our Western society is a task-orientated society. This makes us restless, active, agitated and unable to be still. Although these things are not bad in themselves they do not dispose us to God or to prayer. We see prayer as passive. On the other hand, in places like India, we see people relaxed and motionless; they can sit in prayer and meditation. The impact of restlessness upon our children in Western society is detrimental to any stillness. Our society is also permeated by noise. Yet we know that silence and peace are necessary, so that God can touch our lives.

Our Western culture has buried itself in a mundane worldliness. There is a jail mentality, where we are locked in a dungeon the results of which are despair, boredom and unhealthy patterns of life unsanctified by the light of *wisdom*. We become more and more involved in a secular way of life, so that our world, its peoples, resources and physical energies become things to be exploited for our own selfishness. People then don't feel rooted in God, nor grounded in mystery, but regard themselves as the makers of things – we become creators, but in isolation from *the Creator*. Alienation from the Holy turns to self-alienation. The documents of Vatican II put it thus:

> Ours is a new age of history with critical and swift upheavals spreading gradually to all corners of the earth. They are the products of man's intelligence and creative activity but they recoil upon him, upon his judgements and desires, both individual and collective, upon his way of thinking and acting in regard to people and things. We are entitled then to speak of a real social and cultural transformation whose repercussions are felt too on a religious level.[1]

Yet despite all this there is a search for God deeply rooted in us – longing for the Holy haunts us. This openness is often eroded by Western secularism. The idea of a culture being an obstacle to God is not something abstract but real. We participate in a civilization in which secularization prevails as a way of life.[2]

Any evangelizing process needs to understand the social network at which it is aiming. St Paul changed his strategy wherever he preached. The Gospel is introduced, not into a blank mind but one which is filled with assumptions and interpretations. We need to face issues like secularism head-on. In analysing secularism we need to look at two vital areas, rationalism and materialism. These impinge upon the thinking of every person in the street and influence our culture and indeed our Church.

Rationalism

By rationalism I mean the desire to explain everything through the medium of the intellect. Modern people often lack a sense of God. We then have to fall back upon our minds. Our minds are important to God – that is why any evangelizing will give us 'renewed minds'. But we in the West are struggling with a legacy of rationalism from the seventeenth and eighteenth centuries. Our history books call these 'the Age of Enlightenment'. We have faced an uphill struggle ever since.[3] This age of rationalism put people's mental prowess above God, and I would describe it as a 'second fall'. How did it operate? Basically it saw reason as the only tangible mode of assessment. It reduced the Christian message to rational principles. The Bible was subjected to criticism in order to keep it in line with a reasoned approach. Do not misunderstand me; as an academic myself, I do not decry research or study. My point is that people do not get to God through pure reason. Faith is a gift. St Paul says, 'Make sure that no one traps you and deprives you of your freedom by some secondhand, empty, rational philosophy based on the principles of this world instead of on Christ' (Col. 2:8).

Rationalism makes the assumption that it has reason and science on its side.[4] Christianity can be seen as being opposed to these. The question of truth is one which affects the scientist and the Christian alike. A Christian does not commit intellectual suicide by being a scientist. Trying to face the mysteries of life without reference to the Creator is like trying to tell the time on a clock with only a second-hand.

Science and rationalism are pushing back the frontiers of the unknown, but in most cases the best we can expect from these efforts is to advance the odd mile across a limitless expanse. We need to be open to the supernatural mind.[5] We know that we are something more than a material body controlled by a material brain governed by the laws of physical chemistry. Intellectuals do not have a monopoly of God, nor is God the prerogative of simple or unlettered people. The big question facing our society is, 'Are we prepared to make the journey from our heads to our hearts?' This return journey must also be made.

I am not suggesting here that we should shy away from healthy debate. We need to discuss, reason and debate with the rationalists. We must, however, avoid arguments – these only polarize people. The Catholic Evidence Guild, in the past, discussed and put forward the case for Christianity in public to a largely rational audience. We must not forget those people who speak in public places, like Hyde Park Corner in London, who make a very strong case for Christianity among the jeers of an unbelieving crowd. Rationalism is a strong obstacle to evangelism, but it does not defy dialogue. To the rational mind the word 'mystery' is inexplicable, but to the evangelized mind, the word means a constant unfolding of the truth. One man wrote to me saying that he hadn't slept as a result of one of my sermons. It sent him back to read and research, and this ultimately led him to God. One point we must never forget is that unmovable rationalists are to be found in any of our Catholic congregations as well as outside the Church.

Materialism in society

Materialism, a way of life based upon possessing, permeates our Western society. Materialism and security go hand in hand. It is estimated that between 1950 and the present day, the gross national products of most European countries has risen tenfold.[6] This growth has given countries power beyond flag and nation. Money, and especially the 'oil barrel', has become the bargaining power between nations. We have created an avaricious and greedy people. How blind can our economists be? We have even come to the stage of sharing 'acceptable inequalities' in our attitude to the poor. We are crushing people.[7] Because of the Western world's pursuit of wealth, Third World countries are in danger of becoming economic, social and political casualties.

It is extremely easy to point the finger at the wealthy in

society, but I have found that even those who own very little can also be materialistic if their deepest desire is to gain and accumulate. On them, too, the influence of a secularist society is putting pressure to possess and own. Money makes us comfortable and can even give the impression, albeit subconscious, that God can be bought. In our cities are people known as 'Yuppies', independent people who commit themselves to the attractiveness of possessing. Sometimes it is difficult even for a priest to get his foot across the threshold of their homes. Certainly I have found it extremely difficult to talk about God to these self-made people. I am not singling this group out, but mention them merely as a sign of the times, namely a movement to the right. I preach frequently, to committed Christians as well as others, that 'the last part of us to get redeemed is our pocket'.

After his preaching on the Kingdom of God, Jesus spent more time preaching on the issue of money than on any topic. The Bible has strong teaching on money. Our difficulty is not in understanding but rather our fear of dealing with it. The Gospel *challenges* us to sacrificial action. The word 'challenge' has a military background; to challenge is the duty of a sentry. It is a short sharp question that makes the individual 'stop'. It demands an answer. The biblical understanding of money makes us stop and asks where we stand. 'Do I own my money or does it own me?' There can of course be a right use of money. A giving spirit can enhance the preaching of the Gospel. Jesus walked, talked and dined with wealthy people. This teaches us not to fall into the trap of condemning money. Nonetheless, money is power. It is power which seeks to control and dominate us. Our preaching then in evangelism must call people from attachment to money and into a true worship of God. But we must, first, be free ourselves so that we can show freedom to others. The cost of discipleship is detachment.

Materialism in the Church

The whole area of wealth and poverty in the Church's ranks today is one of great confusion. We, in all good faith, may live a life of detachment, yet we can appear to be very wealthy in the eyes of the world around us. We may be satisfied with the way we live, yet the witness we give mitigates against a true evangelism. We may offer feeble explanations to the enquirer about the relativity of wealth, but this explanation rarely impresses. The reason why people are so attached to Mother Teresa is that she is genuinely poor. I realize that a way of life accepted as poor by one social class would be regarded as well off by others. It has to be said, generally, that an attachment to wealth among modern-day Christians shows that we have not accepted an option for the poor. We have a great problem preaching and witnessing to the poor, because they cannot identify with us. I went to an ordination last summer, where the bishop, in his homily, asked the young candidate for the priesthood to minister with 'an option for the poor'. I felt that this statement was very apt and correct, yet I found myself asking where is the real practical vision for this type of ministry to be executed.

I know that I am putting my finger upon a red raw area in all our lives as Christians. While individual parishes may be struggling to pay their bills, yet in the eyes of the ordinary person in the street the Catholic Church can be seen as wealthy. Any evangelizing that we attempt has no power when the Gospel is not lived. Maybe the problem for us in the Church is that people are no longer expecting us to live the Gospel. No one expects anything different from us. We drive the same cars, live in similar houses and eat sumptuously, just like the wealthy do. We are then at pains to produce evidence that those outside the Church are really missing something that we Christians have. Because we don't have a lifestyle any different from the humanist, atheist, or agnostic, we may resort to gimmicks and aggressiveness. We are reduced to a false salesmanship or showmanship.[8]

All of this begs the question, 'What do we do?' We need to put all our wealth at the disposal of the Kingdom. We need to use it to build the Kingdom. Throwing it away or selling it indiscriminately will not solve the problem. We need to lose the possessiveness we have with regard to our possessions. Bishops, priests, religious and leaders must be seen to be living a simple lifestyle. Believers *are* called into positions of wealth and influence. It is a calling into leadership in all walks of life. Some will be called to make money – lots of money for the glory of God and the common good. What we need to do is help Christians to possess wealth and not be possessed by it. 'The call of God is upon us to use money within the confines of a properly discipled spiritual life and to manage money for the good of all humanity and for the glory of God.'[9]

The 'prosperity gospel'

There are those in the Christian Church who think that the accumulation of wealth is a sign of God's blessings. We call this syndrome the 'prosperity gospel'. This attitude can be expressed bluntly: 'For example Kenneth Hagin, founder of the Rhema Bible Church in Tulsa, Oklahoma, has written that to drive a mere Chevrolet rather than a luxury car is not being humble; it is simply to display one's ignorance of God's law of prosperity.'[10] It becomes a matter of 'choose God and he will make you successful, choose anything else and remain poor'.

This approach to Christianity is not just a warmed-up version of Scripture; it also finds a pivot in the TV and politics of the United States. Rooted in the materialism of the age, the 'prosperity gospel' goes with a popular sub-culture born of TV. Please don't read me wrongly – I believe we should use all branches of the media to get the message of the Gospel across, but this type of TV evangelism has made millionaires of popular preachers. To stay in business they have had to raise the level of 'fund-raising' on the airwaves to an art. In the 'electronic church' giving to the Lord frequently means that the pockets of certain individuals become bigger. Great emphasis is put upon morality, law and order; these are very worthwhile topics but, in the context of the 'prosperity gospel,' they are often seen as strengthening the power of the establishment, the military and the affluent majority. No challenge is issued. Wealth makes us isolated and lonely when no demands are put upon it with regards to the poor.

We must not dismiss this 'prosperity gospel' as a mere flash in the pan. Evangelism has come into people's living rooms, but it remains fraught with danger and is a serious obstacle to true conversion, certainly in a Catholic context. I am in no way decrying other denominations, but I would simply state that down through the centuries the great evangelists in Catholic tradition were also men and women of great poverty – St Francis of Assisi, St John Vianney, St Clare and many more. The first thing that Catholic people will note about their leaders is any disposition to wealth. If a Catholic leader drove up to the door of a church in a Bentley or Jaguar, most of the congregation would not be disposed to hear his or her message. True evangelism does not take political, racial or economic sides, and any attempt at alignment with these will, in the long term, result in barren ground. God is not interested in making individual nations the wealthiest on earth, and the gospel message must never be moulded to suit any narcissistic culture. Conversion must always be proclaimed as a way to the cross; it is not just for ourselves, it is for the world. Evangelizing is not for the poor or the wealthy exclusively – it is about Kingdom values.

Up to this point I have discussed obstacles that face the Church in the world. Now is the time to look at some of the stumbling blocks *within* the Church to an effective evangelism.

Our maintenance mentality

A lot of effort, time and energy are put into buildings. We are often like 'night watchmen guarding a pile of bricks rather than architects instructing workers to put bricks together into a building'.[11] I do not say this to condemn, but rather to highlight a legacy from the past when the Church was seen in an institutional light. The assets of any institution are its wealth and its buildings. As more buildings become redundant in the future, so we have to ensure that ministry is not building-centred but outreach-centred. The tragedy with a maintenance-of-plant mentality is the diminishment of spiritual life that goes with it. We need to view buildings as necessary only as a meeting place for God's people.

Howard Snyder[12] raises the following questions about buildings:

First, buildings are a sign of our *immobility*. The Gospel tells us to 'go' (Matt. 28:19) but our buildings tell us to 'stay'. We are asked to 'seek the lost', but our buildings say 'let the lost seek the Church.'

Secondly, our buildings are a *sign of our inflexibility*. Our Masses, however good, only allow for the direct participation of a few. We are dictated to by the sanctuary layout. Communication is one way, helped by the architecture and the PA systems.

Thirdly, our buildings do not build *community*. With the exception of a few, they are unfriendly places. They often do not facilitate free worship or even good liturgy. They are not designed for fellowship. Homes are, and when worship is expressed in the homes there is warmth and friendship. Maybe this is why there is the upsurge in the 'house church movement'.

Fourthly, our buildings can show a great degree of *pride and class division*. We insist on our buildings being beautiful, and this usually involves great expense. Is it possible that a beautiful building may do no more than attract the rich? Buildings must not produce middle-class values.

However, this is only one side of the coin. It is true also that a cold, dingy unkempt building does nothing to attract people. The setting does help the proclamation of the message.

Some of our best priests and sisters are often given the job of paying off debts. I think that the personnel should be released for ministry, especially in outreach. All the money that we spend on buildings could be better utilized, maybe in training up the people of God. However it is not right to sell our buildings; they must be put at the disposal of the Kingdom. There are competent people around with gifts of administration and maintenance who could look after the buildings – we must not be afraid of losing control. We need to reassess our maintenance programmes for the progress of any evangelistic strategy. We need a missionary spirit not a maintenance attitude.

Over-sacramentalized, under evangelized

The destiny of evangelism is to share the Good News of the Redemption. If we really encounter Christ then we are united with him and through him with one another. We pass with him from death to life. The sacraments are signs of this passage. In our Catholic tradition the substance of the 'eternal covenant' is transmitted to the Church, and in the Church to each of us through the medium of the sacraments. The sacraments are then signs of grace. In the widest sense a sign is something by which another thing is known: smoke is the sign of fire, a scent tells us that the flowers have opened, tracks show the hunter that an animal has passed that way. In a stricter sense, a sign is a thing conventionally used to signify another thing and translate it into terms of the senses, such as the handshake of a friend, the exchange of visiting cards, or road signs. So we understand that the seven sacraments we have in our tradition are signs of God at work within us. Yet it has to be said that every sacrament requires the activity of the receiver (in the case of infant baptism, by a sponsor). Is it possible that some of our people do not have the insight to appreciate the power of these sacramental signs because they are not evangelized?

> In the Christian community, itself, especially among those who seem to understand or believe little of what they practise, the preaching of the *word* is needed for every administration of the Sacraments. For these are Sacraments of faith and faith is born of the *word* and nourished by it.[13]

In recent years there has been added emphasis upon sacramental programmes, especially first communion, confirmation and marriage. Priests and catechists have been endeavouring to hammer home the message to reluctant parents and children. There have been isolated results from these strenuous efforts, but on the whole it has to be said that the majority of people attending these sacramental programmes are left untouched. They usually persevere to 'get it done'. We continue to lay tremendous emphasis upon the sacraments, and rightly so. Sacraments are proclaimed by the Church for special moments in our lives, for significant points in our journey to complete union with God. Baptism with confirmation is the beginning of our salvation. Eucharist completes initiation and provides the ongoing sustenance for our spiritual lives. Orders are the setting aside of disciples for special ministry. The Church exercises the power of healing in the sacraments of the sick and reconciliation, and holds to herself the privilege of solemnizing marriages.

In the history of the Church sacraments are seen not as objective entities but as personal encounters with Jesus. Sacraments are best understood as Jesus reaching out to us, saving us, forgiving us, blessing us, uniting us, consecrating us, empowering us and healing us. Over the years the Church began to emphasize the automatic effect of the sacraments. We call this *ex opere operato* action. Less and less stress was put upon personal response to the action of the Lord. This we call *ex opere operantis* action. We overlooked, more and more, the need for personal response. This, eventually, led to a 'dispensing of sacraments mentality'. The sacramental rituals in themselves were expected to meet all spiritual needs and satisfy responsibility for God's action.

So the question for Catholics is, 'Does the sign convey the gift?' – *ex opere operato*. The objection that I see, practically, is that the majority of our people who receive sacraments are clearly not regenerated into new life in Jesus. Jesus himself warned us of doing all the right things without really coming to know him: 'It is not those who say to me, "Lord, Lord," who will enter the Kingdom of Heaven' (Matt. 7:21).

St Paul also stated that mere external rituals, in that case circumcision, mean little in themselves (Rom. 2:29). What matters is a relationship with God made possible by Jesus. The sacraments should be a 'seal' of this. A person can be baptized, but the effects of this sacrament may not influence his or her life one little bit. The same can be true of all the other sacraments. They can become mere empty rituals performed upon a person with little personal receptivity.

To approach the sacraments efficaciously we need expectant faith. This demands that we be evangelized. There needs to be some sort of covenant relationship between us and God. Jesus is present in the sacraments within the covenant context. The depth of the encounter with Jesus depends on how deeply we enter the covenant. Evangelizing surely means an opening of people to receive. In practical terms this means that the power of the encounter with Jesus, in sacraments, depends on the openness of the individual. Our priests are dispensers of sacraments to, at best, partially committed people. I realize how difficult it is to define or determine commitment. Yet there needs to be some evidence of commitment, otherwise we are merely giving precious diamonds to infants. Preparation for the sacraments is necessary. Adequate preparation will not be achieved by mere catechesis but by asking also for commitment to Jesus and the community. This must not be done in a confrontational way but with love and sensitivity. The delaying of sacraments in certain cases must be an alternative. A common fallacy among Catholics is the administration of sacraments with the hope that a desired result will ensue. This will not happen unless our people are evangelized.

Here I will briefly take the sacrament that is most frequently celebrated by Catholics, the Eucharist. Throughout Europe we have millions of people attending Sunday Mass. I would hazard a guess that a large majority of these people attend because there is a law which says they must. If the law was removed our numbers would drop considerably. We would be left with people who are committed. We have developed excellent teaching on the Eucharist as sacrament and community builder, but in fact the ideal and the real are polarized. We have a large number of unevangelized people in our pews who regularly turn up each week but, realistically, there is very little growth process among congregations from one year to the next. We remain 'much of a muchness'. I believe that the Eucharist is at the centre of our faith as Catholics, but I hear despondent priests asking pertinent questions on how to move their people forward. We have good, generous people, but somehow they are entrenched in a rut that only those who are prepared to be evangelized can rise from. We have the potential for great scope within the liturgy, but yet there is a deadness and complacency. There is lukewarmness of faith among our faithful that can only be rekindled by a new evangelization. Our people need to come alive before our liturgy can be alive. I realize that all sacraments, especially the Eucharist, have the potential for great outreach in the Church. The liturgy of the Eucharist, in particular, can be a tremendous evangelizing force, but only when the congregation look and act as though they are evangelized. We all need to be seen to be redeemed, before any outsider will begin to believe in the Redeemer. The power to evangelize, by an already evangelized community, at Mass is mind-boggling. The same can be true of all the other sacraments when celebrated in public.

In conclusion, I wish to state the power and potential of the sacraments to lead people into a deeper relationship with God. But sacramentalizing an unevangelized person will only lead to further 'dead wood' and 'unproductive branches' in our churches.

> The purpose of the Sacraments is to sanctify [people], to build up the body of Christ and, finally, to give worship to God . . . They not only presuppose faith, but by words and objects they also nourish, strengthen and express it . . . Thus for well disposed [evangelized] members of the faithful the liturgy of the Sacraments . . . sanctifies almost every event of their lives.[14]

Institutionalism

In the gospel story the greatest opposition to Jesus came from the institutions of the day. The Pharisees and the Scribes were dedicated to promote the Messiah's coming, but their system of preparation had become so complete that they no longer left room for the possibility of the Messiah actually being revealed. The gospel story is not just a record of the past but speaks to the Church in each generation. Because of the human nature of the Church, systems have to be devised to keep the Church true to her central mission; hierarchies have to be established to define the various relationships that go to make up the Church; methods of leadership and of communication have to be developed to ensure proper order in the affairs of the Church. These very things can then become a blockage to the purposes of the Church's existence – full proclamation of Jesus as Lord and the ongoing establishment of his Kingdom to the ends of the earth. When the methods, institutions and systems become ends in themselves, they are sources of imprisonment for God's word rather than means to its full, vibrant preaching.

By their nature and definition, institutions will look for and demand success. Results that are measurable are sought and extreme measures are often used to get results. Throughout history the institution of the Church has employed many unjust means to achieve its ends: for example, association with emperors, conquerors, torture, and so on. Admitting mistakes is not part of institutional life, and in terms of the evangelical mission of the Church, this inability to repent of the past is crippling the Church. Sin becomes what other people do and is not readily acknowledged as a reality in the institution.

Security is what institutions want. Things need to be well set up, so that risks are at a minimum and permanence is guaranteed. In the Church, this need for security is seen especially in its clericalism, where control is put into the hands of a few. Even today, when there is so much emphasis on the importance of the laity, direct involvement of non-clerics is regarded as 'helping out' because of the shortage of priests. There is no doubt that the ordained ministry is a vital part of the ongoing life of the Church, but so much of the power of the Church is invested in it that, if there were enough priests, there would be no need for anyone else to be involved. For very many people the Church has become, not the source of power of the redemptive Jesus for the world, but merely a place where very limited services are rendered for human life. The world can be left untouched because the institution is too busy with itself and its upkeep. We can spend time answering questions that no one is asking.

The Second Vatican Council described the Church as a pilgrim people. This denotes movement through the world. It must involve change, adaptation and searching. We need to move with a sense of purpose. However, with a people on the move there is always the strong desire for certainty. Through its institutions the Church has become a teaching rather than a preaching Church. The 'teaching authority' pontificates on so many things with such certainty that the impression is created that searching and questioning are wrong, or at least unnecessary. Prophets have generally been overlooked by their generations even though later generations may canonize them. The energy of the institution is often sucked into self-preoccupation which renders her impotent for the salvation of the world. How much time and effort is put into crossing the 't's and dotting the 'i's so that everything can be tied up in a nice neat package! In many ways the institution of the Church makes the pilgrimage of the Church difficult and laborious.

Any group of talented people who co-operate together over a period of time will, inevitably, be successful. With success comes the automatic temptation of self-interest. Then the purpose of the co-operation changes. This is forever happening in the institutional life of the Church. Young people point to the scandals of the Vatican. This often becomes a convenient tool for shutting themselves off to the Gospel. Religious orders and congregations are probably the clearest example of how vested interests can hinder the free proclamations of the Gospel. Almost all religious orders have been set up to evangelize. Their charism is seen in education and health care, usually for the poor. Each religious order as it grows older becomes more institutionalized, more settled, more wealthy, until the point comes when its members are no longer able to meet the aims of their original founder. Many communities today are facing an identity crisis, in which the greatest part of their struggle is a lack of real freedom in making decisions because of being burdened with possessions. There are too many vested interests, too much to get rid of in terms of wealth and positions, too great a power structure, to allow change for the sake of the Gospel. Of course the same is true of parishes and dioceses. A minimum standard of practice and goodness is established as the norm, because the questions that the Gospel of Jesus raises are often too challenging.

Evangelism is the direct and full proclamation of the Gospel of Jesus Christ. Evangelization is the process of letting his presence be felt in the Church to the point of hope. The pilgrimage of the Church involves constantly changing things that make this proclamation difficult or impossible. The Church will always be made up of sinners, and repentance will always be necessary. If Jesus is truly to be central to the world, then we need to truly understand the world and church situations and be willing to take these on board, so that an effective evangelization can cut across the barriers of secularization, rationalism, materialism and institutionalism. These are but some of the obstacles to evangelism but, to my mind, they are the most pertinent for today.

7

Why Build?

> In the course . . . of history the generation of Christians
> have, periodically, faced various obstacles . . . Nevertheless
> the Church does not feel dispensed from paying unflagging
> attention also to those who have received the faith and who
> have been in contact with the Gospel often for generations.[1]

Sometimes when we talk or write about certain ministries we
tend to lump people together. The Catholic Church itself needs
to be evangelized so that in turn it can evangelize. But just to
make this statement is not good enough. I need to break it
down, so that I can address myself to some of the differing
categories within the Church. 'It has been widely accepted that
Catholics are over-catechized and over-sacramentalized but
under-evangelized. We tend to think that conversion
(*metanoia*) has already occurred.'[2]

I know that there are many types of conversion but Pope
Paul VI puts conversion as, 'a total interim renewal . . . a
radical conversion, a profound change of mind and heart'.[3]

In 1984 George Gallup Jn. made a study of all Christian
denominations, including Catholicism, in the USA, and found
that there was 'very little difference in behaviour of the
churched and unchurched on a wide range of moral and ethical
items'.[4]

Let us now look at some of the areas within the Church and
ask, 'Why do we need to build?'

Why bishops, priests and deacons?

I begin by quoting part of a letter written to me by a brother priest:

> May I start on a personal note. I am a priest and in what I write to you I have tried to gather mostly from looking into my own heart and memory. As a child I was a natural evangelist. I recall a visit one Christmas of a cousin who was not a Catholic. I sat up until 3.00 a.m. telling him about Jesus. That must have been my longest sermon. I was seven years old at the time. In adolescent years I remained evangelically concerned. I went to a non-Catholic Grammar School and enjoyed being given the public-speaking platforms from which I could address 800 fellow pupils and express my Catholic faith. I reckon that in my class of 32 there were four Christians (1 Anglican, 2 Catholics – one of whom was rapidly lapsing – and 1 Non-conformist). So I went to the Seminary. I cannot say that my spirit of evangelism was suppressed or killed – it did not die. But I was in a different world.

Bishops, priests and deacons, we were all trained in Dogma, Philosophy, Scripture, Canon Law, Moral Theology, Aesthetics and Pastoral Theology, yet I, personally, do not recall a single class being given over specifically to evangelization. This academic training should have equipped us to preach the Gospel and made Jesus known to us with a depth of understanding, sincerity and integrity. We bishops, priests and deacons have been taught to distrust enthusiasm. Often our process for discernment in this area is to wheel in the nearest fire brigade and quench the smouldering flax. However, I must be fair to our training, which was done by men with conscientious sincerity. They honestly sought to meet needs. The training they undertook was designed not so much to preach the Gospel as train sacramental ministers, and to place and promote them in this ministry. It was not a training for preaching the joy and freedom of redemption and salvation.

There have been several fundamental changes in the system since I was ordained. I see and like the difference. But this change is not enough; new pressures have arisen in society. A more vocal and active laity has influenced the new model of bishops, priests and deacons they feel they need. They have sometimes tended to make us in their own image and likeness – yes, even while criticizing us for being so. Others have put deep spiritual and psychological pressure on us. We are still not free from the restraints of structure within the framework of what we call 'the Church'. He who preaches the Gospel must have some of the freedom of the Gospel. This requires the confidence and trust of those who commission the preaching and those who hear it.

Bishops, priests and deacons are not unevangelized either. That we have responded to our vocation suggests that this evangelization was not without fruit or effect. Our training was not devoid of evangelism but offered it in such a way as to be fearful and uninspired. We are evangelized but often not adequately. Our evangelization has been neither deep nor mature enough and lacks the means and techniques to evangelize others. Recently, I gave a conference to a number of priests. We talked and shared at length about evangelization. When the week was over, all of them said, 'It is all very well, but we don't now how to do it.'

There has always been an admiration among us for those who have found new ways to evangelize, and sometimes we have shown a degree of envy. I believe this envy is an indication of a deep-down wish to evangelize. We have had so little encouragement.

How many bishops, priests and deacons understand Jesus when he says, 'I have come to bring fire to the earth, and how I wish it were blazing already!' (Luke 12:49)? How many of us can really respond to that?

The question must arise, 'What would happen, what practical results would there be if we clergy were fully evangelized?' The answer requires both logic and imagination. We would be different. We would be men of vision and enthusiasm. The Gospel would be written and expressed in our lives in confidence and we would have a more adult sense of responsibility in freedom. We would have to be sharers in the sufferings of Jesus (we have this already in abundance), but we would also have participation in his Glory. At some stage or another there would be a cracking of our model of diocese and parish. Church life would change. It would mean that we would come into a new understanding of priesthood. This would give us a new security which would allow us to free the laity to exercise their gift of priesthood which was given them at baptism. There would be great resistance to this type of change from both inside and outside the Church, and also from the Devil. But we would gain a new glimpse of the teaching of the Church and in particular of Vatican II.

This will only occur if we use and act upon the word 'conversion'. The gift and time of conversion is the key to it all. Conversion is essential. Without it nothing can happen. If we aim at nothing we will never be disappointed. Responsibility for sustaining and developing conversion is not limited to bishops, priests and deacons, but we can water it or kill it. The growing ground of conversion is evangelization. My friend ended his letter by saying: 'We, as Catholics, talk about the martyrs and dying for the faith. We need to live for it and then our tradition will inspire us.'

Why religious orders – male and female?

> Religious, for their part, find in their consecrated life a privileged means of effective evanglization . . . They embody the Church in her desire to give herself, completely, to radical demands of the beatitudes.[5]

One characteristic of the religious life as it has developed over the last twenty years has been the choice by religious who have the call to the 'working world'. Up to the present, religious congregations have often assigned their members to works of an institutional nature – mostly to colleges, schools and hospitals. These often belonged to the orders or were committed to their care by the Church or State. More and more of these institutions are now being closed, with a result that many religious are confused and are searching around to find an outlet for their charism. Evelyn Woodward puts it like this:

> To take a consciously active role in the shaping of the future is a call to be uncomfortable and displaced. We can no longer be satisfied to operate in institutional ministries however dedicated and laudable these may have been. The call to be pilgrims is louder now than ever before.[6]

In the search for an outlet there arise two dangers. Firstly, there can be a tendency toward excessive self-fulfilment. Secondly, an over-professionalism may be sought. There can also be insufficient public witness and an introspection that can lead to polarization; radical feminism would be an example.

It has to be said that, at a time of greater opportunity for marriage, sexual intimacy, career and wealth, fewer people are entering the religious life. Not many want to live the life of poverty, chastity and obedience. Many are predicting the death of religious life as we have known it. One bishop told me he feels that in time there will be only two kinds of orders left in the Church: the ones who work with the poor and enclosed contemplatives. I tend to agree with him, unless there is a fundamental change and a new evangelization occurs. Witness is the first element that will attract new people. People will not be attracted to religious life if it offers only a partial challenge. The condition for its efficacy in any mission of evangelization has to be a renewed life. How can vows of poverty, chastity and obedience be a prophetic sign to an unevangelized world.

Vows of poverty[7]

Religious poverty is a personal experience. It is a group experience too. And the group significance differs very much from the personal. Religious poverty is also a matter of witness. It may be . . . the most poignant in the eyes of the world.[8]

The voluntary vow of poverty is not a witness unless it involves 'doing without'. It should be possible for people to see this lifestyle as in some way sacrificial. These days many religious talk at length about poverty, but if 'doing without' is mentioned they either avoid it or reject it. Our human instincts say we should 'have'. The outside world can see little or no deprivation among most religious. They can take for granted what the ordinary person in the street has to agonize over – food, security, clothing, etc. By poverty I don't mean here destitution; rather, religious poverty opens people to God and to others and shows the social value of material goods. These need to be put at the service of the poorest and most needy. A new evangelism in this field would dispose religious to use the goods of the earth for everyone's benefit. Maybe we need to fit the lifestyle to the word 'poverty' rather than the other way round.

Vows of chastity[9]

In the past we saw the vows of celibacy as something negative. We renounced the pleasure of sex and marriage. Now we have to see it in a positive light; we say 'yes' to something. We need to see it as a gift despite its cross. The outside world needs to see chastity as a lived experience. We need to work out for ourselves the practicalities of being celibates, so as to free us to be people of love. I know that in the eyes of the world, celibacy can be seen as nonsense. People will ask us, 'How can you do without sex?' At a time when sexual promiscuity is rampant, the Church itself must see us as openly joyful in our celibacy. It is not good enough for most religious to have a theoretical idea of celibacy. When we who are celibate are really evangelized, we will know and experience a deep relationship with God. The instinct for love will become something that unites us closely with God and with each other. Sex and companionship then become a redeeming power. Celibacy is a bond between the celibate and Jesus, radiating out to others as a sign of the Kingdom. We are opened up to wider relationships which are founded on generous love. Celibacy is, undoubtedly, a precious gift and a powerful evangelical sign.

Vows of obedience[10]

Religious obedience is, basically, a communal search for the will of God in union with those who hold authority. Obedience is a human reality. When people live together there arises a need for authority and obedience. Our acceptance of authority is, basically, our acceptance of our place in the group, and this should mean growth. Obedience ultimately demands a gift of freedom. By searching the will of the Father through dialogue, religious life denounces false types of liberty and authority. The witness of obedience entails a freedom to consider the good of others. Good authority is always one of service.

Community living[11]

The call to community by a religious lifestyle should be prophetic for the whole Church. The whole Church is meant to be community, so religious communities are merely microcosms of the Church. Religious communities are called together to share their food, and to work as a team. They pray together and they share their income. Living together they share in the mystery of the Trinity. So community living is itself a witness, because in its very essence it portrays the reality of a triune God. Its witness is evangelistic.

All this shows us that evangelization requires renewed communities of religious. The lived experience of community and the practice of the vows give witness to a consecrated life. These should show the world that their priority is God.

So, far from being a dying breed, religious are going through an immense purification, a pruning which offers a prophetic challenge to the world. Yet religious must always be compelled to examine their lives and endeavour to be a witness, however imperfect, to the reality of God in our society.

Why laity?

Most lay people do not see evangelization as their job. All that is required is to live a good Christian life, to 'keep' the faith, and to leave the rest to priests and nuns who are supposed to be trained for that sort of thing. Evangelization is not in the heart or conscience of our Catholic laity. Faith is still seen as personal and private, and evangelization is regarded as the activity in which over-zealous Protestants engage, grasping people warmly by the hand and asking them if they are 'saved'. I believe that we will never understand our call to evangelize others unless we have first been evangelized ourselves. Our failure to evangelize is one of the reasons why our Church is in decline in the Western World. The teaching that evangelization constitutes the essential mission of the Church, with every baptized person called to play a full part, has not really been understood. We need to know who we are in baptism, to recognize that we form a body with one aim but with different functions, and that we are called to contribute to the health and growth of the Church.

It is all too easy to pass through the full Catholic programme of sacramental initiation without ever being called to a personal faith in Jesus Christ, which is then to be lived out in the Church and in the world. In other words, unless they are evangelized, our churches will continue to be full of nominal Christians, and the number of lapsed Catholics will continue to exceed those who are actively practising their faith. Conversion, I know, is an ongoing process for us all, but we will never change and grow if the primary work of evangelization has not been done.

In today's Church there is over-emphasis on the leader, resulting in shirking of ministry and leaving it in the hands of one person – the priest. This means that priority is given to liturgy and maintenance, rather than to evangelization, and the laity mostly remain at the level of spectators. Lay people are not properly equipped to function effectively; they need motivating, directing, inspiring and training. Unless clergy and laity exist in partnership, we have only a passing membership in the body of Christ. Evangelization is needed to open the eyes of lay people to their place in this partnership. Then we could see that *together* we are the Church – in union with Christ and also in union with his mission to evangelize, which will become our mission too. This vision will affect our whole approach to evangelization.

We can ask, what would be the results if we had an evangelized laity? First, we would have a committed laity, a people committed to Jesus and to each other, with a burning desire to share what they have received with others. We would have a new people, and so, by implication, we would have a different Church. The resulting surge of life and evangelistic zeal among the people would put pressure on the church systems and structures, which would have to change to facilitate this new life. There would be changes in attitudes among the priests and bishops, and full recognition and encouragement of the gifts and skills of the lay faithful as they take their rightful place in the service of the Church. Our lay people would become an encouragement to the clergy, so that their gifts and talents would also be brought forth. Bishops and priests would come alive, and a new pastoring would be envisioned. Instead of fighting for an ear our clergy would begin to teach and lead, and our lay people would be receptive. The old vision of the Church and roles of clergy and lay people would be challenged and a real partnership would emerge. Yes, some priests and people would be left behind, but I'm sure this is inevitable in any growth process. It is not the desire of evangelization to leave people behind but, realistically, it has to be said that some people will not budge an inch.

An evangelized laity would be an evangelizing laity. We would be a people determined to see the Kingdom of God extended and the powers of darkness defeated. We would see the supernatural gifts of the Holy Spirit put to use in demonstrating the power of the Gospel and supporting the proclaimed word. An evangelized laity would seek holiness. We would begin to live values that contradicted those of the world. We would demonstrate gospel values. An evangelized laity would become a socially active people. We would be involved in action wherever there is social or structural injustice. We would speak for those who do not have a voice. Everything in our church life would begin to serve the primary purpose of mission, which stands at the heart of the Gospel, and we would at last be responding to the call of the Holy Spirit to bring the whole Gospel to the entire world. 'Go out to the whole world' (Mark 16:16). Pope John Paul sums it all up when he writes: 'In both accepting and proclaiming the Gospel in the power of the Spirit the Church becomes at one and the same time an "evangelizing and evangelized" community and for this very reason she is made the servant of all.'[12]

Why men?

Pope John Paul says,

Many voices were raised in the Synod Hall expressing the fear that excessive insistence given to the . . . role of women would lead to an unacceptable omission . . . regarding men. In reality various sections in the Church lament the absence . . . of men some of whom abdicate their proper Church responsibilities, allowing them to be fulfilled only by women.[13]

Across all denominations, the present Christian Church in Europe has a proportion as high as two women to one man. It is a reality that has to be faced. Imbalances tend to perpetuate themselves, and in a society where the image of men is macho, heroic, self-confident and self-sufficient, religion can be seen as an unmanly thing to be involved with. Because of the predominance of women going to church this is seen as a woman's thing. Men will agree that religion is good for setting morals, but when it comes to the kids, the wife looks after that side of things. I realize that these are generalizations, but for too long the Catholic Church has failed to get its hands dirty in reaching out to working men. Although the hierarchy is male-dominated it has done little to attract men. There is a need to forget religion and 'churchy' things and concentrate on presenting Jesus to men.

The problem needs to be tackled realistically, with determination and adhering to basic principles. To single out men will demand a new strategy for evangelizing them, apart from all the present programmes. How many men are received into our churches through our present programmes? Men do not like mixed meetings and are likely to be embarrassed in front of women. Men may be frightened, feel pressurized, experience emotional turmoil and be in need of healing and counselling, but social convention says they cannot express these feelings or needs openly. This means that in evangelizing men we need to plan carefully where we meet them, so that we begin in comfortable surroundings. Traditionally we have said that the way to a man is through his stomach. Maybe we could try men-only breakfasts and suppers with a speaker who is well-known – a sporting, television or political Christian personality. Pubs are where we find most men. Could we have a room in a pub, have a bit of food and a good speaker? We could hold the breakfasts in the church hall but the suppers, ideally, need to take place in a local hotel or restaurant. Non-Christian men would be accompanied by a Christian friend who, if necessary, would cover the costs for themselves and those they bring.

Sporting events can also be a way of reaching men, Christians playing alongside non-Christians. But, as with any event of this kind, Catholic men need to witness to their faith. Catholic organizations, like the Knights of St Columba, St Vincent de Paul, the Catenians and Catholic Men's Society, have tremendous potential for reaching out to men, but they must do it in a positive way if it is to be effective. Existing organizations and groups should be utilized wherever possible, but only if they are open to becoming involved in the proclamation of, and witnessing to, their faith. Men need to start praying that God will give them contacts with fellow Catholics and non-Christians, opening the ways for witnessing to Jesus.

Men are basically activists. The Church needs to utilize its males in areas where they have gifts, encouraging and supporting them constantly. We have lost working men in the past; now we need to look at this area and provide support for working men. We also need to provide the basic means and motivation for Catholic men in the pews to be morally aware and capable in their working situations where there are increasing pressures to immorality. In terms of our preaching we must encourage men in their family responsibilities. Men need to exercise the authority that God has given them, taking a full part in the upbringing of their children by being an honest and commendable witness to them and their mother.

Women can have a tremendous influence on men. They can be very active in sharing the Gospel with a lapsed or uninterested husband. Not all men are religious, but on the whole husbands do not hinder their wives from believing. I know many husbands who drive their wives and kids to Mass on Sunday. It may be a good idea for a wife to say occasionally, 'Why don't you come to Church today with me and the kids?' but not too often. It's not good to pester. A woman should always keep her husband in the picture about what is going on at church, looking out for special events in the church to which she can invite him. She can pray for men and particularly for her husband, share with him and encourage him.

If the Church is not going to become a place for nice old ladies on Sundays while the men stay at home, then it has to act quickly and decisively. We must aim at evangelistic strategies for men as readily as we do for young people.

Why young people and Catholic schools?

Ask any parish priest about the needs of his parish and pretty near the top of his list, if not at the top, will arise the issue of young people. Our problem is not so much what to do with them but rather the search for them. The age gap in congregations is widening each day, and those whom John Paul II called 'the Church of today, the hope of tomorrow' are fast becoming the 'godless of today and the lost of tomorrow'. We are groping in the dark as to how to find them.

In addressing this problem we must begin by asking ourselves, 'What have we offered our young people?' To be more concrete, what has been the experience of 16-year-old Catholics faced with the personal choice of making Catholicism their own? They have been baptized, confirmed and have gone to Mass with their parents, probably for years. They have had dozens of RE lessons and said many prayers at school. The religious lessons and prayers cease when they leave school. From then on going to Mass is the only tangible link with the Catholic Church, but they rarely feel part of the Sunday liturgy. I know that some young people have good experiences of faith and are well integrated into the parish, through prayer groups and good catechesis, but action is needed if we are going to make this the rule.

Such action, it has been said, has been and is taking place through the Catholic educational system. If this is the case, why are there not more young people in our pews? Where are the fruits of school labours? I know that there are a variety of pressures on our Catholic school staff (educational, economic and administrative). Teachers feel overburdened and undervalued. We are grateful to those teachers, both Catholic and non-Catholic, whose continued dedication to their work gives such a fine example of committed service. However Catholic education is at a cross-roads. Are our Catholic young being offered a Christian education by evangelized staff? Do our schools wish all the students to come to a personal knowledge of Jesus?

Some would say that removing the emphasis of 'Catholic' from a school would be a way forward, partly because it would focus people on the issue of how the local church as a body is reaching out.[14] We have for years taken for granted that the Catholic school is keeping young people centred on Jesus. Evangelization and catechesis belongs to the community of believers. Perhaps in Catholic schools we have attempted to catechize those who were unevangelized. We are then disappointed when the young stop going to Church in late teenage years. How can we expect a person to enter the house of someone they don't know?

So what do we do? We need to introduce our young to the living person of Jesus in a loving, joyful and effective way. We need to offer them Christ as a way of life. To communicate Jesus in this way will mean utilization of relevant resources, be it good rock-music which carries the gospel messages or effective dynamic and faith-evoking preaching which reveals a God of young people. It will mean a fresh look at liturgy, for this should always bring joy and a sense of celebration into each Eucharist.

Young people respond to challenges. Every day our young are bombarded with sights and sounds inviting them to become more sexually active, to drink, to smoke, to make money and to look after 'number one'. Do they also see and hear an equally inviting challenge to say 'no' to these things and to make Jesus Christ the person whom they wish to follow? Are they being challenged to decide to carry the cross and be different? Recently I was asked to preach to a group of 17- and 18-year olds. I challenged them to be different and to stand and make a commitment for Jesus. All of them responded bar three. This challenge can only come from a Catholic Church which is committed to continual conversion in Jesus. Let us allow them to see, hear, touch and know a Jesus who has risen out of the religious education books and into their lives.

Why ecumenism?

> The power of evangelization will find itself considerably
> diminished if those who proclaim the Gospel are divided
> among themselves in all sorts of ways.[15]

In some ways the greatest problem we face when trying to
evangelize those outside the Church is the ever-present issue
of the divided Church. People can quite legitimately say to us,
'When are you going to get your act together?' or 'What branch
of the Church do you want me to belong to?'

How do people know who is telling the truth. We are following in the footsteps of Jesus' mission, namely to proclaim the
Gospel. When we bring the Good News to a world afraid and
lonely in its pain, surely we also should proclaim a Gospel that
transcends past divisions and calls all to the one Almighty
Father. We cannot do this with integrity if our evangelizing is
sectarian in its aim. We surely must serve a higher aim than
that of building up a particular church or denominational
group. Our aim must be the growth of the Kingdom and the
building of the body of Christ both inside and outside the
Catholic Church. Such an ecumenical vision is vital if we are
to respond to the Pope's appeal to evangelize.

There is a form of tribalism in our Western Church. It is a
legacy of the Reformation and counter-Reformation. We are
crippled by denominationalism – the great divide between
Catholic and Protestant. This remains an open wound in the
body of Christ. Yet this very division could, by a strange para-
dox, witness to the glory of Jesus if we would respond to his
call to demonstrate a genuine ecumenism that reaches across
the divides. Think of the impact if we truly joined forces to
proclaim the Gospel while continuing to know and grapple with
the deeply held convictions that divide us. What a testimony
to the glorious power of Jesus to draw people into one body
across man-made barriers! Only a gospel proclamation that
comes from costly reconciliation and genuine ecumenism in

action can provide such an authentic voice. We are all preaching reconciliation between God and people. People will only believe this when they see it in action. At present our actions deny our words, and we are found to be unauthentic. Lord have mercy on us.

Some may say that I am naively overstating my case. Yet what are we to make of the words of Jesus, 'With me in them and you in me, may they be so completely one' (John 17:23)?

Our denominational differences may in their variety reflect the wonderful diversity of humanity. Can anyone doubt that our suspicions of each other, pride in our traditions, our stubborn refusal to work together and, in some places, even a poisonous hatred of each other, continue to break the heart of God? Yet since Vatican II the 'Catholic Church has recognized our separated brothers and sisters as somehow participating in the reality of Christ's mystery on earth through their faith and sacramental life.'[16]

Our foundation surely must be our baptism as Christians. We use the term 'our separated brethren'. In spite of a common baptism our separated brethren remain as separated as ever. Europe needs to see that Catholics mean business in the ecumenical field. We are part of the same Christian family, even if some family differences have arisen. In ordinary families these things happen. But it need not stop us from enjoying family celebrations together. Such events should take place at every level, national, diocesan, metropolitan, town or parochial. Even if the day of shared eucharistic celebrations is still far off, at least we can demonstrate in other joint celebrations how much we long for the day of eucharistic unity.

How profound also it would be to see an evangelist of the Protestant tradition and a Catholic priest stand together on the same platform, sharing the preaching as fellow missionaries. It would be a symbolic gesture of prophetic nature in which the Gospel proclaimed would be dramatized by the very act of proclamation. Our evangelism surely must be ecumenical, otherwise it denies the power of the message it spreads. May

God give us the grace and the courage in boldness that the whole Church may be delivered from the bondage to ancient conflicts and the Gospel seen for what it is – a reconciling power.

8

Building Blocks

The world around us is becoming increasingly secularized. People are less receptive to approaches in evangelism that have been effective in the past. We need some practical guidance in the process of evangelism. My desire here is to communicate principles which will serve as a basis for action. Methods can only be applied in specific contexts. At the end of the day evangelism involves living in a dynamic relationship with Jesus and this cannot be stereotyped. Evangelism is, by its nature, flexible. My purpose, therefore, is not to write a 'how manual' but merely to provide ideas so that these can be adapted by individuals and communities.

When Jesus gave us the great commission, 'Go make disciples of all nations . . .' (Matt. 28: 19–20), he did not tell us how to do it. We were commissioned and sent to evangelize, but not given the methods for the task. Could one of the reasons why the disciples were so afraid and fled to the upper room be that they were apprehensive about this command given by Jesus? Throughout the gospels Jesus rarely, if ever, tells us how to do the work, just that we have a responsibility to do it. If he had given us a blue-print we would probably still be slavishly focusing on his methods, methods that were effective for the people of his day two thousand years ago. While not negating in any way the principles described in chapters 4 and 5, we need to develop methods that are effective for *our* world. We must take initiatives. Even though we are inadequate and our gifts for action under-developed for the task, we need to be encouraged by the words of Jesus, 'Know that I am with you always; yes, to the end of time' (Matt. 28:20). After all, God blesses steps taken in faith.

Where there is no action there is, basically, nothing to bless. Nothing is happening. We need to display an aptitude for action that will take priority over sending out masses of analyses and papers through 'talk shops' and committees. Reports on findings do not, in my opinion, spur us into action. The Catholic Church is not short on mission theology; what is needed is to transfer our allegiance from maintenance theology to *missionary action*. While theory and tools for the job are important, we must now realize that the time is ripe for the next step – ACTIVITY. We need to look upon ourselves as 'marketing people' for today's Church. In a letter to the Bishops of Europe (January 1986) Pope John Paul II urges the Church to go out and 'sell' itself. European society has entered a new phase of its historical progress, and there is a 'need for a new quality of evangelization'. Jesus used three words: 'go', 'teach' and 'make' (Matt. 28:19–20); these are all active verbs.

> The question of 'how to evangelize' is permanently relevant because the methods of evangelizing vary according to the different circumstances of time, place and culture, and because they thereby present a certain challenge to our capacity for discovery and adaptation. On us . . . rests the responsibility for reshaping with boldness and wisdom, but in complete fidelity to the content of evangelization, the means that are most suitable and effective for communicating the Gospel message to the men and women of our times.[1]

So there is no single style in evangelism. There are as many styles as there are evangelizers. This diversity is important, because those whom we are trying to reach are many. Each one of us has backgrounds and techniques that appeal to certain people. No single one of us can do the whole task but, working together, we can build the Kingdom. However we must be careful not to confuse the messenger with the message: Jesus' mother Mary was a messenger; Jesus is the message. 'There is no true evangelization if the name, teaching and life of Jesus of Nazareth are not proclaimed.'[2] The effective messenger is always faithful to the authentic message. We are 'ambassadors for Christ' (2 Cor. 5:20).

It is important at this stage to reflect upon some principles which are fundamental to our efforts to evangelize.

Witness of lifestyle

What we communicate to people by example is more important that what we communicate to them verbally. 'Actions speak louder than words' is a phrase I believe we all use. We have all heard brilliant orators in our time, but what matters is not the nice silver words tripping off the tongue, as from a car salesman, but rather the lived experience. Mere empty words make us no more than 'resounding gongs or clashing cymbals' (1 Cor. 13:1). A declaration without a lifestyle to back it up is meaningless, even counter-productive; the language of evangelism surely has to be the language of 'love'. If we demonstrate by the way we live and relate to others that the love of God is a reality in our experience then, surely, it is most difficult for people to walk away untouched.

I could write endlessly on how this love can be shown in practice. It could be meeting crisis situations with and for others. It could be offering help to the less fortunate. It could be as simple as offering a cup of cold water. It could be shopping for someone in need. The list is endless. There are thousands of little ways to show the love of God in our everyday lives – we need to be available to care. Caring, loving people cross the threshold of cynicism and hardness of heart quicker than thousands of sermons. Our actions can open up channels of communications, or close them, quicker than anything else. Loving actions show others of what we are made. There is little likelihood that a person will take us seriously unless he or she can be assured that our words and actions arise out of conviction. Nor will we be taken seriously if there is any indication that we are not authentic. If we show a person a nettle and say that it is a rose, we must not be too surprised if our words flow in one ear and out the other. If Jesus is not a reality for us then there will always be something unauthentic about our message. Evangelism has to be incarnational for it to be authentic. The early Church turned the world upside down by its lifestyle. Is it possible that the world has turned our churches upside down? I believe that our problem lies in the fact that we are witnessing to a secondhand Christ of doctrine rather than a first-hand account of a Jesus we have experienced.

The evangelizer's love of God applied to concrete situations is absolutely essential for effective evangelism. The trouble with most people in our churches, today, is that they find it difficult to believe that God loves them. When they cannot experience this tremendous love that God has for us, it makes it almost impossible to give any of that love away. After all, we cannot live or give away what we really haven't got. It is no wonder, then, that the world is suspicious of the Jesus we offer. People can sense if our faith is genuine. If our deepest relationship is with God it will be seen in all our actions. We must not fall into the trap of thinking that the 'good news' we bring is going to automatically get us a hearing. We have to earn our audience. This means building relationships, and to build relationships we must associate and identify, in love, with people. 'The first means of evangelization is the witness of an authentic Christian life, given over to God in a communion that nothing should destroy and at the same time given to one's neighbour with limitless zeal.'³

Recently, at the end of a conference which I gave, a man came up to me and said, 'Father, all this evangelizing business is great, but I do it by the way I live.' This comment is very frequent in our Catholic tradition. If I had a penny for each time it has been said to me I would surely be a millionaire. This type of comment can be used as an easy 'cop-out' phrase. Basically, it means that we have heard of the exhortation to spread our faith but we are going to do nothing further about it. Maybe we feel that we are doing it already, but if we are witnessing by our lifestyles, then why aren't our churches full? Is it possible that the lifestyles we live open up areas of conversation but, somehow, we are unable to follow this up? How will people ever know what empowers us unless we have the courage to tell them about Jesus. We can witness by our lifestyles but then fall down on what to say.

On the other hand, maybe, our resorting to 'witnessing by the way we live' is a way of escape for us. Maybe we really don't want to let people know the way we live, because our lifestyle is scarcely distinguishable from the society around us. The lifestyle of most Western Christians and churches offers little prophetic challenge to an increasingly agnostic or even atheistic society. Is it possible that we have quite unconsciously adopted the values and standards of the world around us? If we, the body of believers, dared to live a gospel lifestyle, it would probably be the single most powerful evangelistic step we could take. I realize that we can never be perfect, but at least we can open ourselves to be constantly challenged by gospel values. Then we can begin to take little steps in mutual encouragement towards a full and prophetic way of living.

In the evangelizing community to which I belong the greatest witness given to people is by the lay members of the community. That is not to say that the priests and religious in the community are bad witnesses, but people tend to expect it from us – it is seen as our 'job'. When outsiders see that 'ordinary lay people' have given up security, jobs, prospects for promotion, etc., then they take notice. The question asked frequently of members of our community is, 'Why are you doing this work?' This gives us an opportunity to witness to Jesus.

I am not suggesting that everyone who reads this book should give up jobs, security or homes. We all need to assess how we are living and what witness, if any, is portrayed to the world around us. Witness by lifestyle, 'involves saying how I translate my faith into daily living . . . We have to discern with those with whom we share our faith how it should affect our lifestyle.'[4]

The witness of lifestyle most offended against in our culture is in the areas of power, sex and money. It is not possible here to deal adequately with these, so I hope that readers will be open enough to assess their lifestyle with these headings as guide-lines. These three areas throw us into the arena of moral choice. Christians need to look realistically, though not exclusively, at power, sex and money to assess what it means to live faithfully as a follower of Jesus. These are the areas that most affect Western society. If we, as Christians, endeavour to use these correctly, then we shall certainly be noticed as people with different ethical standards.

Today, we need a new articulation of Christian 'vows'. Such vows will constitute a new call to obedience to Christ in the midst of contemporary society. The need is great. The task is urgent. Our century longs for a new demonstration of joyful, confident, obedient living. May we be just such a demonstration.[5]

Preaching

They will not believe in him (Jesus) unless they have heard of him, and they will not hear of him unless they get a preacher. (Rom.10:14–15)

We live in a society of slick communication, a society bombarded by words. A child growing up today may well spend years of his or her life watching television. Despite the increase in literature, it is the spoken word that still influences the vast majority of people. Preachers are competing with the media for an audience and often becoming disillusioned in the process. Nevertheless to preach the Gospel is not merely to say words but to effect a deed. To preach is not just to stand in a pulpit and speak, no matter how eloquently and effectively, nor is it to set forth a theology, no matter how worthy or how clearly it is stated. To preach is to become a part of a dynamic event, wherein the living, redeeming Jesus reproduces his act of redemption in a living encounter with people through the preacher. True preaching brings the living reality of Jesus to life for the hearer.

So the first principle for good preaching is that the preacher is convinced and lives what he or she preaches. Eloquence, literacy finesse, logical arrangements, sustained progression, the personal appeal of the preacher, handsome appearance, intellectual brilliance, profundity of thought, the ability to sway an audience – these are but accidents, not the essence of preaching. One could have all of these and yet not preach. I'm not discounting these qualities; they can certainly enrich the effectiveness of a preacher. But the authentic word of God, true preaching, may come through a poor preacher if he is already evangelized. Introducing God to people through sincere preaching is a most valuable way of evangelizing our people in the pews. No person has truly preached until the two-sided encounter between the preacher and the congregation has given way to a three-sided encounter where God himself becomes a living party to it. Preaching is the act through which 'saving facts' are reopened in the experience of people now.

I am an ardent believer in the importance of preaching in our churches. It is indispensable both for evangelization and for the healthy growth of the Church. 'The contemporary situation makes preaching difficult: it does not make it any less necessary.'[6]

Like many other preachers, I do not consider myself an expert on preaching. I often leave a preaching or proclamation situation dissatisfied, feeling that I have been unable to really communicate what has been 'burning' inside me. There may be two reasons for this: (a) my own inadequate preparation, tiredness or whatever; or (b) the people to whom I am preaching are unreceptive or unevangelized.

Here I would like to offer priests some words of encouragement. For some priests preaching is a disillusioning experience.

We can make the mistake of preaching instruction to an unev-angelized audience. This will mean that the words from our mouths do not find a home in the people. They bounce back and choke the next words coming from our lips, so that we may flap around trying to find an inroad to where the people are. Some people come to our churches with a desire to be entertained rather than to gain food and teaching to build up and equip themselves for the week ahead.

Priests are also often at a disadvantage when they try to explain the Scriptures to people in their homilies. We can be fighting a losing battle, because the majority of Catholics are not very familiar with the Scriptures. In the General Instruction of the Roman Missal we read, 'In the Mass both the table of God's word and the table of Christ's Body are prepared.' So for explicit explanation of the Scriptures to take place during the sermon, our people must somehow become soaked in the Scriptures from which will develop a desire to be evangelized and in turn evangelize.

One weekend, while working in London, I took time off to visit a city centre church for midday Mass on the Sunday. The Church was full to capacity but somehow there was an unwillingness on the part of people to hear what was a very good sermon. People were looking at their watches, eager to get away. On this occasion proclamation of any kind would have fallen on deaf ears.

However, the poor quality of Catholic preaching is a cause for defection from the Church. The churches that are growing today are churches where preaching is taken seriously. There is an attractive magic in a good preacher. This attractiveness comes with earnestness and a zeal to proclaim the Gospel, and energy enough to have prepared the message with proper care. In a time of uncertainty and confusion the preaching that we hear needs to be basic, uplifting and stimulating. The demands made upon priests (I'm not suggesting that only priests can preach) these days, has made it impossible for them to prepare adequately. I have found also that a fear of failure in preaching stops people from really proclaiming the message. We need always to keep at the front of our mind that the call to faith does not rest on human wisdom but on the power of God (1 Cor. 2:5).

Preachers must work hard to produce food for the people. At times of weddings, baptism, funerals, etc., there is a greater openness in people to receive – even among those who are non-churchgoers. The sermon needs to be presented in such a way that all are able to receive it. If it is pitched at the right level it will edify all in the congregation. We must try to avoid all words which are not easy to understand – simplicity is attractive. The preacher must know, as far as possible, the needs of the congregation. After my ordination an old priest said to me, 'If you want to preach effectively to your people you need to knock on their doors and visit them.' There is truth in this statement, because the best preachers that I've heard are the ones who visit their people. We understand the needs when we listen at the grass-roots of the Church. The renewal of a dynamic preaching must be linked with the renewal of the Church. If the Holy Spirit is alive in a congregation it will evoke the charism of preaching in the preacher. If the preacher is alive he or she will disturb a sleepy congregation. We must remember that, today as ever, 'the verbal proclamation of a message is, indeed always, indispensable'.[7] We need to rediscover a confidence in the proclamation of the Word of God.

Catechetics

The definitive aim of Catechesis is to put people not only in touch but in communion in intimacy with Jesus Christ. (Pope John Paul II)[8]

Catechetics can be a powerful way to evangelize. If catechizing is done well we can evangelize at a deep level. We have developed, over the last decade, powerful and effective programmes, especially with regard to the sacraments. Let us consider the tremendous input that teaching can have on parents as their children prepare for the sacrament. Parents are always open to having their children receive the best, and these parents will do almost anything that is asked of them that can be helpful to their young. One big reason, lately, for a large number of adults returning to the practice of their faith has been through the catechetical preparations set up for their children. Parents want religious education for their children and they want to set a good example for their child. They may be inactive Catholics, but at that time they are often ready to welcome a person who reaches out to help them – even in a challenging way. Realistic help must mean an invitation to respond with a deeper personal faith. One of the major ways used by the Jehovah Witnesses and the Mormons is their detailed attention to instruction. They will even bring videos and overhead projectors into people's homes to help with instruction.

It has been my experience that in catechizing situations I have found a great lack of evangelizing. Priests, teachers and catechists endeavour to teach or impart faith as they would teach any academic subject. While realizing the content must always be present in a teaching programme, it will be ineffective if the person imparting the knowledge is not convinced of what he or she is teaching. The first thing we look for in teachers and preachers is whether they are really convinced themselves about what they are saying. Have they a living relationship with Jesus? Good catechesis pre-supposes an evangelized catechist. Some would even say that catechetics builds upon an already evangelized person. 'Evangelization begins when the individual is in some way challenged by the Gospel. Only when this initial step has been taken can catechesis properly begin.'[9]

I believe it is both. Good catechesis can dispose a person to evangelization and at the same time fan into flame an existing spark of faith. 'Touched by Grace [the person can] discover little by little the face of Christ and feel the need of giving themselves to him.'[10]

Catechetics must always lead people to conversion. The clearest expression of this is seen in the Rite of Christian Initiation of Adults (RCIA). It tells us that catechesis is the result of conversion and also leads to it. RCIA makes it clear that catechesis is connected to conversion.

There must always be content in catechesis. People need to know what to believe, so information is important. If, however, catechesis does not evangelize – leading to commitment and conversion – something is missing. It will not fulfil its promise unless it evangelizes. There is also a crying need in our churches for ongoing teaching. Remember, we have a responsibility to those whom we evangelize. Teaching is of immense importance for Christian maturity. In my opinion the Catholic Church is great when someone is searching for God, but when a person has been evangelized we are not too good at the follow-on process. We often just leave them at the level of 'Mass-goers', and they then get lost in the crowd. We need a consistent programme for discipling people into living communities.

Using the media

'The Church would stand guilty before Our Lord if she did not use these powerful means.'[11] These strong words, about the mass media, are from Pope Paul VI. He goes on to say that by using the media we can reach the 'multitudes'. It is possible in the USA to switch on the radio or the television set and to hear the direct message of the Gospel expounded. Even some Catholic dioceses have their own stations. Satellite TV time is being bought here in Europe by major Christian companies in the USA. I, personally, have great reservations about this type of Christian broadcasting but, nevertheless, it has made an impact upon people's lives and it will not go away. Ignoring it, or just being critical of it, will not affect its impact.

Few would deny the media's power. It is a vehicle for expressing ideas, and is commercial and consumer-orientated. Certainly, Catholics here in Britain and Ireland, must not regard it with a *laissez-faire* attitude, but become involved. Although some work is being done, I think it is fair to say that there is great reluctance on the part of Catholics to do even simple things like articles for newspapers, or interviews on radio stations. We must not be left behind or allow the media to ignore us, or else to show us as irrelevant. Christians are frequently caricatured as fuddy-duddy, with heads firmly in the clouds and feet off the ground. Rarely do we see a character in a soap-opera with a real, living Christian faith. It is even rarer to hear or see a programme which sets out to explain the gospel message in simple language. On early morning TV breakfast shows the 'horoscope slot' is put over in an appealing way. So could we not agitate to hear a 'prayerful slot' at the beginning of each day? We already have this on some of our radio stations.

Recently I was invited to take part in a two-hour programme on a British radio station. When I arrived at the studio with my Bible the producer said to me, 'You are not going to quote that over the air?' My comment to him was that I am a Christian and wish to speak as one. An Irish broadcasting station asked me to prepare something on marriage. When I did so, they refused to let it go out over the air because it contained definitive Christian teaching on marriage. These are isolated cases, but it is true to say that producers often want a message that will not disturb or challenge the listener or viewer.

The general public needs to see and hear what Christians are doing. We need programmes that challenge the false gospels of the secular world. People need to see worship that is genuine and joyous and relaxed. There are churches where hundreds of young people attend, and every practising Christian should be made aware of this, if only for encouragement sake.

The advent of cable TV in Europe could weaken the Catholic Church and cause a lot of people to leave us. We need to meet this problem creatively and produce programmes of good quality, so that we have a reasonable chance of 'reaching out'. I believe that it is right for us to relate with artists who work on video, TV and radio. The same with newspapers; let us put our talents to work and inundate the press with 'good news' so that a positive approach of hope may be read in our papers.

First, we must not be scared of the media, but learn to understand it. We should ask ourselves, 'What contribution am I making to the media in my area?' Local radio and press are good starting points for sharing what is happening in our own patch. Evangelism through the media is a great priority, and we need to make sure that we have Catholics working in this field – and support them in prayer and encouragement. Pope John Paul II exhorts,

> . . . all those who have at heart the Apostolate of Communication to give themselves with ardour and energy, and with due respect, to every person to the great work of evangelization.[12]

One-to-one

> Side by side with the collective proclamation of the Gospel, the other form of transmission, the person to person one, remains valid and important.[13]

Over the last thirteen years I have been privileged to listen to many people relating the story of how they found Jesus or came into a deeper relationship with him. This personal story or testimony is vital in evangelism. While rallies, conferences, preaching and teaching do bear fruit, the one-to-one sharing of faith is more effective. People usually respond favourably to the Gospel in the personal and unthreatening situation of one-to-one sharing.

We may be afraid of sharing on a one-to-one basis because we think that people will have a bad opinion of us. But a simple willingness and readiness to share with others about our Christian faith is an essential ingredient in one-to-one evangelism. When new Christians are asked what drew them to the

Church, the most common answer is 'another person'. They are often invited to come to Mass and this begins the process.

One-to-one situations are available to us all. Whatever our situation in life or our job of work we come into contact with people in the course of our everyday lives. I'm not suggesting 'pushy-ness' but a simple openness to situations. Occasions, if we are sensitive, will arise for us to witness. We all have to be aware of the opportunities for evangelizing that surround us. I personally find, while travelling on buses, trains, planes, or even when I pick up a hitch-hiker in the car, that situations arise into which I can speak. When we do talk about faith on a one-to-one basis, we often discover a 'lapsed' Catholic. We probably meet at least three or four times as many unchurched people as churched ones. These are all our brothers and sisters with whom we can share the Good News. No, I correct myself – these are fellow human beings to whom we owe the Gospel. When we hesitate, we need to ask ourselves, 'Why?' They are probably saying, 'Why not?'

To speak on a one-to-one basis we don't need to be theologians; all we need to be is ordinary. We do need courage, and to take risks. 'The degree of our security in our relationship with God is in equal and direct proportion to the degree in which we are willing to take risks.'[14]

One-to-one evangelism does not require years of training. We, in Sion Community, have found, however, that when we train people in the techniques, it enhances their expertise and usually bears greater fruit. Even without training each of us can do it in our own way. Effective evangelizing does not require extraordinary skills and comprehensive training. I would say that the first attribute we must have is to be open and natural, and then to have a very simple willingness to share.

There must be no aggressiveness or artificiality. Many people consider their faith to be a very private affair, almost a spiritual confidentiality. We need to understand that Jesus called us to be 'lights in the world' and 'salt of the earth'. A wise Christian will sensitively be a 'light' and witness on a one-to-one basis with fellow workers, neighbours, friends, students, etc. If we move in aggressively on unsuspecting listeners, they will only crawl away and probably avoid us in the future.

Here are seven suggested ways to make our one-to-one witnessing productive:

(1) We must meet people where they are on a social level. If we don't meet people as they are, how can we introduce them to Jesus?

(2) We need to establish a common interest, in order to build a bridge of communication.

(3) We need to arouse interest in our listener, to kindle their curiosity.

(4) Let us give only as much of the message as our listener is ready for. Many of us want to rush in and rattle on. People need time and can only take on board so much.

(5) We must not condemn. Any degree of condemnation will appear to be rejection.

(6) We must not get side-tracked by red herrings or controversial subjects. These serve only to alienate or polarize.

(7) We need to speak directly of Jesus. Vague theology or discussions about the Church may sometimes serve a worthwhile purpose but do not necessarily sow the seeds of the Kingdom.

These are seven simple principles which can be used to churched and unchurched people alike. Once we begin to use them we shall move out in faith. We can watch for opportunities which God will send our way, and we shall overcome any reticence that is in us. Many good Catholics say to me, 'I'll stuff envelopes or lick stamps, I'll even hand out hymn books, but please don't ask me to talk to people about Jesus.' A large majority sit back and let the 'pros' or the gifted people do it, while the Gospel continues to be little known and even less believed. A one-to-one approach can stop this trend. It can help us in all sorts of situations. It can assist and enable us to be good listeners and sharers in the pub, at the school gate and the supermarket, with children and youth, with the retired and the bereaved, with single people, married couples and a host of others. 'What is first needed for the evangelization of the world are those who will evangelize.'[15]

Discipleship

Whatever style of evangelizing is adopted it must be blessed by the Church. The bishops and priests need to get behind it in a practical way so that long-term results may be achieved. We are not evangelizing just for our own generation but so that a legacy of good fruit can be left behind for our children and their children. Future generations will judge us in the same way as we judge past generations. I pray that history books of the future will praise us for our willingness to say 'yes' to Vatican II and, in particular, to *Evangelii Nuntiandi* of Pope Paul VI.

The evangelization work of the Church cannot be left to people on the fringes; it must be adopted by the main-line Church. I realize that there are many things wrong with our parish system. Yet people must be evangelized into it; they cannot be evangelized into a vacuum. Maybe, if enough people in the Catholic Church become evangelized, this itself will change the structures. Some say that we could not cope with an influx of new converts – they would swamp us. However, fringe evangelism would create a fringe church and then, ultimately, a split would occur. We already have enough churches, but not enough adequately evangelized people.

A productive structure within the parish system needs to be found to facilitate the evangelized. In any evangelizing process follow-through, or discipling, is vital. Continual personal contact is necessary for encouraging discipleship, and this can only be adequately achieved in small groups. Karl Rahner said before his death that the Church will again 'become the little flock'. He meant that we will only grow strong in small groups.

In his book *Successful Home Cell Groups*[16] Dr Paul Yonggi Cho describes how the small-group system has made his church the largest single Christian congregation in the world.

For those who are lapsed, or those outside the Church, a church building is threatening and uncertain ground. The home isn't. My own experience has taught me that the average person is apprehensive and afraid of coming into a church environment. So, instead of being confronted by a large building, people could be taken into the comfort of a living room. This will set them at their ease and dispose them to discipleship in a small-group setting. The 'house-church' movement is an attestation to this vehicle of discipleship.

In the small discipleship group doubts can be handled and fear erased. The problems of peer pressure is lessened and discouragement abated. Both new and not-so-new Catholics may set very high standards for themselves, and when they fail to meet these standards they may get disheartened and depressed. The Lord can strengthen such people, but often that strength comes through the insights and help of Catholic brothers and sisters.

The strength of cell groups is in the creating of little communities. Vibrant little communities could make our Sunday congregations rich with life. In the cell-group system we can be sure that we are following Jesus and not playing religious games. Christianity, when all is said and done, is about relationships – our relationship with God, his with us, and our relationships with others. Discipling people is essential if any worthwhile building is to be achieved. I know it will be difficult and painful, but it will also be fruitful. 'It is as we seek together to deepen our knowledge of the Son of God that we shall grow in spiritual unity and maturity and thus reveal something of the glory of the fullness of Christ.'[17] This discipleship process is attained in small cell groups. Catholics need to take this seriously to supply dynamism and growth in personal and church life.

These then are some of the building blocks which are necessary in the edifice of restoration. Building in evangelization is both possible and practical.

Conclusion

Sure foundation – hope

This book has focused on the essential mission of the Church – evangelism. I would like to think that you are stimulated now to action and are beginning to ask the question, 'What can I do?' I hope that I have given enough guidance to get you started.

You may have felt as you read the book that I have raised more questions than I have answered. Certainly I have raised questions about the implications of our reaching out to those in the pews and also to non-churchgoers.

My purpose in writing was to repay the debt I owe to the Catholic Church by being raised to the priesthood in these wonderful days. However, the debt we all owe the Church is to put into action the practice of evangelizing. I pray that the greatest thing I shall have brought through this book is hope for the future. Our hope lies in an evangelizing Church.

The devil loves to play the discourager. The work of building the Kingdom is tough. Catholics are not immune from the depression which can affect the whole of society, but we must not let a mood of apathy and despair settle over our Church. I am aware of the immense privilege of Christian ministry entrusted to our Church in these days. We need to bring the message of love and mercy in evangelization to broken people. What the prophet Isaiah is saying to us is so relevant: 'No need to recall the past, no need to think about what was done before.

See, I am doing a new deed, even now it comes to light; can you not see it?' (Isa. 43:18–19).

The greatest mistake we can make is to believe that the activity of God in the West has been exhausted. New acts of God will happen in our Church over the next ten years, the Decade of Evangelization. It will go far beyond anything that people can accomplish or deserve. My hope is that people will rise to the challenge. We need to bury our indifference, so that our Church can be renewed and reformed. Then it will convey the light brought by Jesus – into the third millenium. As in the past there will be false teachers and teachings. Some people see little reason to be optimistic, and maybe in human terms they are right. Yet divinely speaking, with new hope, Christians can change the course of world events.

The following quotation sums it all up: 'One hopes that every day we are conscious of our privilege and duty to announce Jesus Christ to all people, by what we say, by what we do, by the lives we lead and even by the kind of people we are.'[1]

Let us hold fast to our future hope. Let us be aglow with fervour as we build the Kingdom.

References

Chapter 1: A Church Reconstructed

1 Vatican II, *The Decree in the Church's Missionary Activity*, Section 1.
2 Pope Paul VI, *Evangelization in the Modern World* (1974), section 14.
3 Ibid, section 15.
4 Ibid.
5 Michael Green, *Evangelism Then and Now* (Inter-Varsity Press 1983), p. 13.
6 David Watson, *I Believe in Evangelism* (Hodder & Stoughton 1979), pp. 25–6.
7 Tom Forrest, in *New Evangelization 2000*, an international magazine (Rome 1987), no. 1.
8 George G. Hunter, *Contagious Congregation* (Abingdon Press, Nashville, 1984), pp. 26–8.
9 S. Eliot Wint (ed.), *Evangelism Strategy for the 80s* (Pickering and Inglis 1980), pp. 42–3.
10 Pope Paul VI, op. cit., section 17.
11 J. Cumming and P. Burns (ed.), *The Church Now* (Gill & MacMillan 1980), p. 24.
12 Pope Paul VI, op. cit., section 71.
13 Carl Jung, *Modern Man in Search of a Soul* (Ark Publications 1985), p. 235.

Chapter 2: Solid Foundations – The Basics

1 A very helpful book on the basics of the Christian faith is Ian Petit, *The God Who Speaks* (Daybreak/Darton Longman & Todd 1989).
2 David Pawson, *Truth to Tell* (Hodder & Stoughton 1977), p. 14.

3   Karl Rahner (ed.), *The Encyclopaedia of Theology* (Burns & Oates 1975), pp. 4–13.
4   Ibid., p. 341.
5   Ibid., p. 343.
6   John Richards, *But Deliver Us From Evil* (Darton Longman & Todd 1974).
7   Vatican II, *Church In The Modern World*, section 13.
8   Kenneth Boyack (ed.), *Catholic Evangelization Today* (Paulist Press 1987), pp. 38–9.
9   Pope Paul VI, *Evangelization in the Modern World* (1974), section 22.
10 David Watson, *I Believe In Evangelism* (Hodder & Stoughton 1976), p. 74.
11 Vatican II, *The Church In The Modern World*, section 22.
12 Pope Paul IV, op. cit., section 27.
13 A team of St Paul's Sisters, *The Faith We Live By* (St Paul's Edition 1969), p. 62.
14 Pope Paul VI, op. cit., section 75;
15 Ibid., section 10.
16 Ibid., sections 8 and 9.
17 Ibid., section 10.

Chapter 3: Building on Rock

1   Material in this section is derived from Leon Dufour, *Dictionary of Biblical Theology* (Chapman 1978), pp. 486–9.
2   Ibid., pp. 489–91.
3   Anderson & Stransky (ed.), *Mission Trends*, no. 2 (Paulist Press 1975), pp. 24–44.
4   Pope Paul VI, *Evangelization in the Modern World* (1974), section 42.
5   Ibid., section 1.
6   Leon Dufour, op cit., pp. 490–1.
7   Karl Rahner (ed.), Encyclopaedia of Theology (Burns & Oates 1975), p. 292.
8   Sherwood Eliot Wint (ed.), *Evangelism – Strategy for the 80s* (Pickering and Inglis 1978), p. 28.
9   Material in this section is derived from (a) Leon Dufour, op. cit., pp. 215–17; and (b) J. L. MacKenzie, *Dictionary of the Bible* (Chapman 1976) pp. 320–3.
10 Pope Paul VI, op. cit., section 12.

11   David Watson, *I Believe in Evangelism* (Hodder & Stoughton 1976), pp. 26, 32, 34.
12   J. I. Packer, *Evangelism and the Sovereignty of God* (Inter-Varsity Press 1986), p. 40.

Chapter 4: The Master Builder – 1

1   Pope John Paul II, *Christifideles Laici* (1989), paragraph 35.
2   R. E. Coleman, *The Master Plan of Evangelism* (Power Books 1972).
3   Asbury Smith, *The Twelve Christ Chose* (Harper Books, New York, 1928).
4   *The Way*, Supplement 63 (The Way Publications, Autumn 1988) pp. 14–24.
5   Josemaria Escrivan De Balaguer, *Christ is Passing By* (Veritas Publications 1974), pp. 18–20.
6   E. F. Schumacher, *Small is Beautiful* (Abacus 1983).
7   Larry Christenson, *Back to Square One* (Kingsway 1980), pp. 59–65.
8   Yves Congar, *Jesus Christ* (Chapman 1968), pp. 107–27.
9   David E. Roseage, *Climbing Higher* (Servant Books), pp. 27–32.
10   Finbarr Connolly cssr, *Religious Life* (Reality, Dublin, 1985), pp. 48–50.
11   A. M. Hunter, *Introducing the Christian Faith* (SCM Press 1984), p. 81.

Chapter 5: The Master Builder – 2

1   Gerard Egan, *You and Me* (Brooks/Cole Publishing 1977), pp. 3–21.
2   John Haughey, *The Conspiracy of God* (Image Books 1976), p. 12.
3   Pope John Paul II, *Christifideles Laici* (1989), section 7.
4   Daniel Ange, *Les Saints de l'an 2000* (Editions Saint Paul 1981), pp. 98–122.
5   *Florida Catholic*, 13 March 1987.
6   *The Catholic Evangelist* (USA), Nov./Dec. 1985.
7   *The Word Among Us* (Scripture Monthly Magazine, USA), January 1989.
8   Vatican II, *Decree on Divine Revelation*, section 25.
9   J. N. M. Wijngaards, *Communicating the Word of God* (Theological Publications, Bangalore, 1979), p. 34.

10 A. W. Tozer, *The Holy Spirit is Indispensable* (reprint leaflet of Alliance Witness).
11 Gene Hunter, *The Contagious Congregation* (Abingdon Press 1979), p. 128.
12 Pope John Paul II, *Christifideles Laici* (1989), section 22.
13 E. M. Bounds, *Power through Prayer* (reprinted Moody Press, Chicago), p. 7.

Chapter 6: The Stumbling Blocks

1   Vatican II, *Church in the Modern World*, section 4.
2   Bryan Wilson, *Religion in a Secular Society* (Watts Publications 1966).
3   E. E. Hales, *The Catholic Church in the Modern World* (Image/ Doubleday 1958).
4   John Macquarrie, *Principles of Christian Theology* (SCM Press 1966), pp.1–35.
5   Anthony Kenny, *Reason and Religion* (Blackwell, Oxford, 1987).
6   Daniel Yergin and Martin Hillenbrand (ed.), *Global Insecurity* (Penguin 1982), p. 2.
7   Richard De Lamarten, '*Big Blue: IBM's Use and Misuse of Power*' (Pan 1988) p. 254.
8   Jim Wallis, *The Call to Conversion* (Lion 1971), pp. 18–37.
9   Richard Foster, *Money, Sex and Power* (Hodder & Stoughton 1985), p. 46.
10 *The Tablet* (3 Dec. 1988), p. 1388.
11 Michael Harper, *Let My People Grow* (Hodder & Stoughton 1977), p. 24.
12 Howard Snyder, *New Wineskins* (Marshall Morgan & Scott 1987), pp. 61–5.
13 Deretz and Nocent (ed.), *Dictionary of the Council* (Chapman 1968), pp. 381–2.
14 Vatican II, *Constitution on the Sacred Liturgy*, sections 59, 61.

Chapter 7: Why Build?

1   Pope Paul VI, *Evangelization in the Modern World* (1974), sections 50, 54.
2   Susan Blum, *The Ministry of Evangelization* (The Liturgical Press, Minnesota, 1988), p. 26.
3   Pope Paul VI, op. cit., section 10.

4 George Gallup Jn., *Religion in America*, The Gallup Report, no. 222 (Princetown NJ 1984), pp. 18–19.

5 Pope Paul VI, op. cit., section 69.

6 Evelyn Woodward, *Poets, Prophets and Pragmatists* (Collins/ Dove 1987), p. 3.

7 Material in this section is derived from F. Connolly, *Religious Life – a Profile of the Future* (Reality, Dublin, 1985), pp. 60–8.

8 Ibid., p. 60.

9 *Signum Magazine* (5 Feb. 1988), vol. 16, no. 2, pp. 10–11.

10 UISG (International Union of Superiors General) Bulletin (1982), no 59, p. 8.

11 J. Tillard OP, *Dilemmas of Modern Religious Life* (Dominican Publications 1986), p. 29–30.

12 Pope John Paul II, *Christifideles Laici* (1989), section 36.

13 Ibid., section 52.

14 Sheila Kelly, 'Catechesis and Religious Education in the Roman Catholic Secondary School: a Philosophical Study' (M.Ed. thesis, University of Liverpool, May 1988).

15 Pope Paul VI, op. cit., section 77.

16 *New Dictionary of Theology* (Gill & Macmillan, Dublin, 1987).

Chapter 8: Building Blocks

1 Pope Paul VI, *Evangelization in the Modern World* (1974), section 40.

2 Ibid., section 22.

3 Ibid., section 41.

4 Patrick Purnell SJ, *Our Faith Story* (Collins 1985), p. 98.

5 Richard Foster, *Money, Sex and Power* (Hodder & Stoughton 1985), p. 15.

6 John Stott, *I Believe in Preaching* (Hodder & Stoughton 1982), p. 9.

7 Pope Paul VI, op cit., section 42.

8 Pope John Paul II, *Catechesis in Our Time* (St Paul Publication 1979), p. 9.

9 J. Gallagher, *Guidelines 86: Living and Sharing Our Faith – a National Project* (Collins 1986) p. 12.

10 Pope Paul VI, op. cit., section 44.

11 Ibid., section 45.

12 Pope John Paul II, 'Religion in the Media', World Communication Sunday, 7 May 1989.

13 Pope Paul VI, op. cit., section 46.

14 Susan Blum, *The Ministry of Evangelization* (Liturgical Press, Minnesota, 1988), p. 49.
15 Pope John Paul II, *Christifideles Laici*, section 35.
16 Paul Yonggi Cho, *Successful Home Cell Groups* (Logo International 1981).
17 David Watson, *Discipleship* (Hodder & Stoughton 1981), p. 60.

Conclusion

1 *Venerabile*, magazine of the English College, Rome (1988), vol. XXIX, no. 2, p. 76.